Just the Facts

Introduction *to* Soil Science

Second Edition

National Agricultural Institute

Published by:

National Agricultural Institute, Inc.
151 W 100 S
Rupert, ID 83350
USA
(208) 957.7000

ISBN 978-0-578-14182-4

To learn more about the National Agricultural Institute visit:

www.national-ag-institute.org

Or visit us on Facebook: www.facebook.com/NationalAgInstitute/

Send comments or questions to: info@national-ag-institute.org

Notice to the Reader

Table of Contents

Preface

This textbook, Introduction to Soil Science, is one in a series of *Just the Facts* (JtF) textbooks created by the National Agricultural Institute, representing a bold, new approach to textbooks. These textbooks present the essential knowledge in outline format. Essential knowledge is supported by a main concept, learning objectives, connection to national agriculture, food and natural resource (AFNR) standards and key terms, at the beginning of each section. Content of the books is further enhanced for student learning by connecting with complementary PowerPoint presentations and websites through QR codes (scanned by smart phones or tablets) or URLs. Instructors and students will find the extensive table of contents useful for planning class presentations and getting to important topics. Each textbook is available in print and electronic formats.

The time is now for a new mindset about textbooks. Textbooks for the future need to take advantage of both print and digital technology, while keeping costs down.

Just the Facts series of textbooks provides a synergistic textbook model - print and digital working together to be better than either one alone. Moreover, in a time of increasing costs for textbooks, print copies of Just the Facts textbooks are priced substantially less than traditional textbooks.

The first of these new textbooks also includes:

- Just the Facts: Introduction to Agriculture
- Just the Facts: Introduction to Animal Science
- Just the Facts: Introduction to Biology
- Just the Facts: Introduction to Food Systems Science
- Just the Facts: Introduction to Plant Science

Other titles scheduled for release as a part of the Just the Facts textbook series includes: Introduction to Agribusiness; Introduction to Sustainable Agriculture; Introduction to Aquaculture Science and Introduction to Equine Science. More are in the planning stages.

Instructors using one of the textbooks for a class of 15 or more students are eligible to receive the complementary PowerPoint presentations, laboratory activities and final assessments.

Just the Facts textbooks are a project of the National Agricultural Institute, Inc. created, written and assembled by:

Rick Parker, PhD, President
Marilyn Parker, Vice President
Karen Earwood-Kenny, Board Member and Assistant Editor
Miriah Pace, Board Member and Assistant Editor

1 Importance of Soil

Major Concept

Soil is an important natural resource, providing a medium for plant growth and in turn furnishing food for humans and animals.

Objectives

- List three factors affecting soil creation
- Identify the composition of soil
- Name three ways soil is important for plant growth
- Outline three cycles that involve the soil
- Identify two agricultural and two nonagricultural uses of soil

Key Terms

- Adobe
- Carbon cycle
- Concrete

- Hydrologic (water) cycle
- Load-bearing capacity

- Mineral cycle
- Nitrogen cycle
- Shrink-swell potential
- Soil

Chapter Resource

Complementary *full color* illustrations, photos, charts and graphs are available by scanning this QR code or by following this URL: https://www.tagmydoc.com/SS01 These digital resources will enhance your understanding of the chapter concepts.

Soil Definition, Composition and Formation

- **Soil** is the soft material that covers the surface of the earth and provides a place for the growth of plant roots.

  o It is composed of mineral particles, organic matter, water and air.

  o The long-term health of agriculture, and of human society, depends on the health of the soil – one of the most important natural resources.

  o Atmosphere, crust and soil interact to provide plants and animals with the needed resources to live and thrive – proper temperature, water, carbon and other nutrients.

- Soil is created through a variety of processes and over long periods of time.

  o Factors affecting soil creation are: parent material, time, climate, organisms and topography.

  o Decomposed plant and animal material add to soil.

Soil Characteristics for Plant Growth

- Climate

  o Affects soils by causing physical and chemical weathering of rock – the main effects due to temperature and rainfall.

  o Affects amount of plant growth and therefore amount of organic matter added to soil.

- Gases

  o Includes nitrogen (N_2), carbon dioxide (CO_2) and oxygen (O_2).

- Water

  o **Hydrologic cycle** (water cycle) continually moves water from the soil to the plants then to the atmosphere and back to the soil.

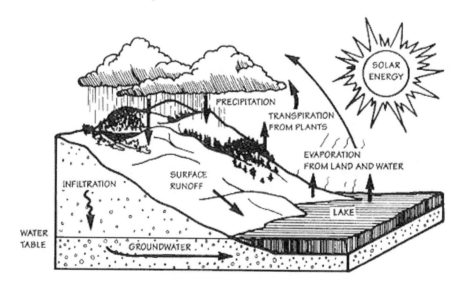

- Carbon (C)
    - **Carbon cycle**: Plants remove carbon dioxide from the atmosphere and oceans by fixing it into glucose; in turn, animals, plants and human activities produce carbon dioxide (CO_2) by respiration, decomposition and burning which is used by photosynthesis.

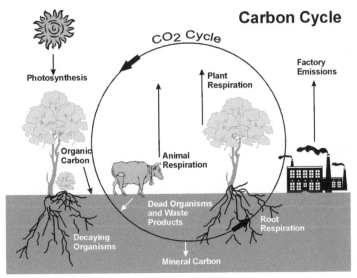

- Nutrients
    - Plant nutrients cycle through the soil in two kinds of cycles - nitrogen and mineral.

    - **Nitrogen Cycle**
        - ✓ This is the movement and exchange of organic and inorganic matter back into the production of living matter.

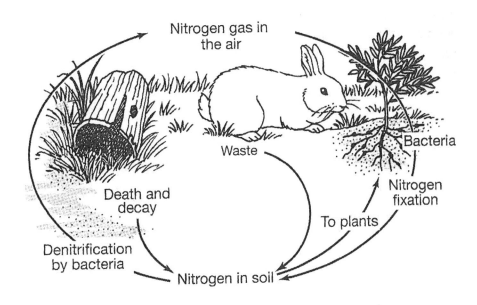

o Mineral Cycles

   ✓ Organic matter decomposes, releasing minerals for uptake by plants.

   ✓ Cycles include phosphorus, sulfur, potassium and other minerals important to plant growth.

Soil - Medium for Plant Growth

- Plants depend on soil for three needs: water, oxygen and nutrients.

   1. Water

      ✓ Plants obtain water through the soil into their root system.

      ✓ Available and unavailable water in the soil is determined by the water-holding capacity of the soil.

   2. Oxygen

Chapter Resource

      ✓ Required by all living plants and animals.

      ✓ During photosynthesis, plants release oxygen and then consume it during respiration.

      ✓ Plants have easy access to oxygen above ground; underground, roots and soil organisms use oxygen and release carbon dioxide.

      ✓ To sustain adequate oxygen for plant roots, soil aeration exchanges soil and atmospheric air.

   3. Nutrients

      ✓ Carbon, oxygen, nitrogen and hydrogen are non-mineral nutrients needed and are available from water and air.

      ✓ Twelve other nutrients are needed as macro- and micro minerals.

Agricultural Uses of Soil

- Cropland

   o Includes areas used for production of adapted crops for harvest. Two subcategories recognized are: cultivated and non-cultivated. Cultivated cropland comprises land in row crops or close-grown crops and other cultivated cropland, for example, hay land or pastureland that is in a rotation with row or close-grown crops. Non-cultivated cropland includes permanent hay land and horticultural cropland.

- Grazing Land

    o Collective term used by the USDA-Natural Resources Conservation Service (NRCS) for rangeland, pastureland, grazed forestland, native and naturalized pasture, hayland and grazed cropland.

- Forest

    o Those ecosystems that have a tree crown density (crown closure percentage) of 10% or more and are stocked with trees capable of producing timber or other wood products. This includes land from which trees have been removed to less than 10%, but which have not been developed for other uses. They can include deciduous trees, evergreen trees and mixed land.

- Other Uses

    o Greenhouses are being used worldwide to grow crops year-round because of the ability to control growing conditions.

    o Soil used for landscaping in a variety of settings, helps to conserve soil, and may continue for many years, requiring different management techniques.

Non-Agricultural Uses of Soil

- Engineering

    o Testing and modification occurs before any construction.

    o Structurally sound buildings are dependent on the skill of the builder and the soil on which it stands.

    o **Shrink-swell potential** is extent that a clay (smallest class of soil particles) soil will expand or contract when wet or dry) and **load-bearing capacity** (what soil is able to support) are critical factors in the construction of buildings and highways.

- Recreational Facilities

    o Require knowledge of soil properties to build areas that will enhance the facility and preserve the soil.

    o Sport-playing fields are challenging because they require special mixes of loam, specific sand size and other ingredients. These recreation/playing fields have several soil layers and are carefully maintained.

- Waste Disposal

  o Soil is a treatment that filters out some materials from human waste.

  o Microorganisms break down organic parts into less dangerous compounds.

  o Sewage treatment plants handle end products by spreading on soil as a source of nutrients and organic matter.

  o Hazardous waste landfills require soils that will not allow leaching into water tables, lakes or streams.

- Building Materials

Chapter Resource

  o **Adobe**, a mixture of sand, clay, water and sometimes a fibrous or organic material, has been used for buildings for thousands of years.

  o Earth, used in the construction of underground houses, houses built into hillsides and houses constructed of packed earthen walls.

  o **Concrete**/Cement – Concrete is a fine powder made of limestone, silicon, aluminum, iron and clay and mixed with water. When water is added, cement hardens.

Summary

Soil is the soft material that covers the surface of the earth and provides a place for the growth of plant roots. It is composed of mineral particles, water, air and organic material. Soil is created through a variety of processes and over long periods of time. Soil characteristics are affected by climate, gases, water, carbon and nutrients. The water, carbon, nitrogen and mineral cycles affect plant growth also. Plants are dependent on water, oxygen and nutrients in the soil. The water, nitrogen, mineral and carbon cycle all affect soil which affects plant growth. Agricultural uses of soil include crop, range and forest lands. Nonagricultural uses of soil include recreation, engineering, waste disposal and building materials.

Additional Resources

Gregorich, E.G. and M.R. Carter. 1997. Soil quality for crop production and ecosystem health. Burlington, MA: Elsevier Science.

Parker, R.O. 2010. Plant & soil science: Fundamentals and applications. Clifton Park, NJ: Delmar, Cengage Learning.

Plaster, E.J. 2013. Soil science and management. 6th ed. Clifton Park, NY: Delmar, Cengage Learning.

National Resources Conservation Service
http://www.nrcs.usda.gov/wps/portal/nrcs/main/national/soils/health/

Soil and Water Conservation Society
http://www.swcs.org/

Soil Science Society of America
https://www.soils.org/

Assessment

 Take the online assessment here: https://goo.gl/EruuHR
Download and print the expanded written assessment by scanning this QR code or by going to this URL: https://www.tagmydoc.com/Ch01SS

Notes:

2 Soil Origin and Development

Major Concept

Soil is formed by the ongoing, dynamic and active processes of physical, chemical and biological weathering of rocks. The factors of parent material, time, climate, organisms, topography and human interventions influence soil formation.

Objectives

- Define pedology
- Name two types of weathering
- List the five soil-forming factors and give examples of the effect each have on soil formation
- List the three broad types of rock and give one example of each
- Define soil profile
- List two soil horizons and their contents

Key Terms

- Alluvial fan
- Alluvial soils
- Biological weathering
- Chemical weathering
- Colluvium
- Deltas
- Eolian deposits
- Floodplains
- Frost wedging
- Glacial drifts
- Horizons
- Leaching
- Levees
- Pedology
- Pedon
- Residual soil
- Root wedging
- Salt wedging
- Soil horizons
- Soil profile
- Talus
- Weathering

Chapter Resource

 Complementary *full color* illustrations, photos, charts and graphs are available by scanning this QR code or by following this URL: https://www.tagmydoc.com/SS02 These digital resources will enhance your understanding of the chapter concepts.

Study of Soils

- **Pedology** is the study of the formation and classification of soil.

  o Pedology deals with: pedogenesis, soil morphology and soil classification.

  o A soil's history can be determined by a **pedon** – a unit of soil, typically one meter by one meter in width and 1.5 meters deep (extending to the root depth).

Formation of Soil

- All soil begins with solid rock. Forces of nature since earth began millions of years ago, such as wind, running water, rain, earthquakes, landslides and other forces have changed rocks into soil. These changes occur very slowly. Soil is still being formed today.

  - **Weathering** – The process by which rock is broken down into smaller pieces.

    - ✓ Physical weathering (sometimes called mechanical weathering) is the disintegration of rock by physical forces such as temperature, water, wind, and other factors. No change to the chemical nature of the rock occurs.

    - ✓ **Frost wedging** occurs in cold climates when water freezes and expands in rocks. The action of expanding and contracting causes the rock to crack peeling outer layers away (exfoliation).

    - ✓ **Salt wedging** occurs when salt is left behind after water evaporates and over time the salt creates pressure causing rocks to split and weaken.

      Frost Wedging

      Water-filled crack   Freezes to ice   Breaks Rock

    - ✓ Swift moving water can pick up and drop rocks, causing them to break or experience physical change.

  - **Chemical weathering** occurs when changes in the chemical makeup of rock is altered causing it to soften and/or break down. This type of weathering occurs mostly in hot and humid environments.

    - ✓ Oxidation occurs when the oxygen in water combines with metallic elements in rock to form oxides (rust). The resulting oxide is weaker than the original substance. For example: A rock containing iron will become red or rust color when oxidized.

    - ✓ Hydrolysis occurs when rock minerals chemically combine with water to produce different compounds and minerals. For example, feldspar crystals in granite can react with rain and become chemically altered to form clay minerals (which weaken the rock).

    - ✓ Carbonation occurs when carbon dioxide dissolves in water, creating carbonic acid which decomposes rock. This process is important in the formation of caves. For example: mineral calcite, commonly found in limestone, is washed away by carbonation, hollowing out rock and thus creating a cave.

  - **Biological weathering** occurs when plants and biological life contribute to the disintegration of rocks.

✓ **Root wedging** occurs when roots grow into a crack in a rock and the pressure of this pries apart the stone.

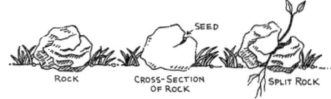

ROCK   CROSS-SECTION   SPLIT ROCK
            OF ROCK

✓ Lichens, a moss like substance found on the surface of some rocks, is a composite organism (emerging from algae and/or cyanobacteria) that has a symbiotic relationship with fungi. Lichens dissolve rock and also leave small cavities that can hold water that then freezes and thaws leading to further weathering.

✓ Burrowing animals can cause weathering by moving rock fragments to the surface. The rock, in its new placement, is exposed to different elements and processes.

Rocks and Minerals

- Rocks are the solid, unweathered material of the earth's crust; classified into three broad types: igneous, sedimentary and metamorphic.

    1. Igneous rock (examples: granite, basalt).

        ✓ Most of the earth's crust is igneous rock overlain by sedimentary rock.

        ✓ Created by the cooling and solidification of molten materials from deep in the earth (molten magma).

Large intergrown crystals

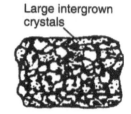

        ✓ Contain minerals that supply 14 of the required plant nutrients.

    2. Sedimentary rock (examples: limestone, sandstone).

        ✓ Overlays about three-quarters of the igneous crust.

        ✓ Formed from sediment deposits when loose materials (mud, sand) are deposited by water, wind or other agents.

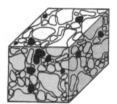

sedimentary rocks

        ✓ Is slowly cemented by chemicals or pressure into rock.

    3. Metamorphic rock [examples: marble (formerly limestone), quartzite (formerly sandstone)].

        ✓ Formed when igneous and sedimentary rocks are subjected to great heat and pressure.

Marble

✓ Soils that come from a metamorphic parent material will resemble soils from the original sedimentary/igneous rock that it came from.

Soil Formation Factors

- Five factors influencing soil formation are: parent material, time, climate, organisms and topography. *Human activities can be considered a sixth factor as most soils have been changed by human influence.*

1. Parent Material

    ✓ Refers to rock or other material from which soil is formed.

    ✓ Influences formation of soils by rates of weathering, nutrients held, and particle sizes contained.

    ✓ Can either form into soil in place or deposit soils elsewhere (transported).

    ✓ Soil that is formed in place is called **residual soil**. Residual soils: weather in place, weathering occurs slowly, are shallow and usually found on bedrock.

    ✓ Usually material is transported to another location before it becomes soil. In these instances, parent material is transported by many means including water, gravity, wind, ice and volcanic activity.

2. Time

    ✓ Soil needs time to form and become richer in organic matter; components are constantly changing.

    ✓ Nitrogen levels increase with time.

    ✓ As soil ages, it forms distinct layers, called **horizons**.

    ✓ Eventually soils become leached and more acidic.

Chapter Resource

3. Climate

    ✓ Warmer temperatures, humidity and lots of rainfall speed up soil formation and tend to create richer, deeper soil.

    ✓ Cooler temperatures with less precipitation slow down soil formation.

    ✓ Climate also impacts degree and speed of initial weathering on rocks.

4. Organisms

 ✓ A small fraction of soil is comprised of living and dead life forms.

 ✓ Roots from plant life create passages for ants, earthworms, rodents and snakes, who in turn dig and till the soil.

 ✓ Plants and animals provide nutrients in the form of their waste products and their dead bodies.

 ✓ Micro-organisms help decompose materials, adding richness to the soil.

 ✓ Plants drop their leaves and recycle ions to plant roots.

5. Topography

 ✓ The shape of the land surface, its slope and position on the landscape, have a great influence in how soils form.

 ✓ The steepness of a hill or a slope will impact how quickly erosion takes place (wind and water carrying away surface soil).

 ✓ In flat areas, soil will usually have deeper, more mature soil layer, as there will be less erosion.

 ✓ Drainage is increased or decreased based on how well soil is able to get rid of extra water. If a location becomes water logged, oxygen will be blocked, hindering soil formation.

- Means by which parent materials are transported:

 o Parent materials are commonly transported away from their original location before becoming soil via the following means:

 ✓ Water – **deltas** form from rivers flowing into oceans depositing sediments at the river's mouth.

 ✓ **Alluvial soils** are deposited by fresh running water, such as rivers, which form sediments. An **alluvial fan** is a fan-shaped sediment deposit usually found at the base of a mountain range or hill.

 ✓ **Levees** are ridges of sediment deposited naturally alongside a river. These can be through flooding or manmade to regulate water flow.

 ✓ Floodwaters spread over large flat areas are called **floodplains.**

- ✓ **Leaching** – Dissolved substances can pass through soil by rainwater or irrigation, which causes the loss of water-soluble plant nutrients.

  o Gravity

    ✓ **Colluvium** is material that slides/rolls down slopes (land slide).

Chapter Resource

    ✓ **Talus** is sand and rocks that collect at the foot of a slope.

  o Wind

    ✓ Wind-transported parent material is called **eolian deposits**.

    ✓ Loess soils or wind deposited silt is very fertile.

  o Ice

    ✓ Glaciers move picking up and transporting soil, rocks and debris.

    ✓ Melted glaciers leave deposits called **glacial drifts.**

    ✓ Particles reached glacier lakes and formed lacustrine deposits on lake bottoms.

  o Volcano

    ✓ Ash blown out of a volcano and carried by wind.

Organic soils vs. mineral soils:
All the above transported materials are mineral soils which contain less than 20% organic matter. Organic soils contain 20% or greater organic matter. These are formed under the water as aquatic plants die and pile up. When the lake fills in, organic soil is created.

Soil Profile

- A **soil profile** is a vertical section of soil from the ground surface downwards through all of its horizons to where the soil meets underlying rock. Whereas, a pedon is the whole three-dimensional section removed; the soil profile is what borders each side of the pedon, thereby showing the vertical horizons or layers.

  o Four soil-forming processes:

1. Additions: Materials such as fallen leaves, wind-blown dust, decomposing vegetation and organisms or new material deposited by wind and water.

2. Losses: Materials are lost through movement of wind or water or uptake by plants, soil particles such as sand, silt, clay and organic matter, or chemical compounds can be eroded, leached or harvested from the soil, changing the chemical and physical composition of the soil.

3. Translocation: Movement of soil within the soil profile and/or between horizons; materials are altered in the soil by organic matter decay, weathering of minerals to smaller particles or chemical reactions.

4. Transformation: The chemical weathering of sand and formation of clay minerals, transformation of coarse organic matter into decay resistant organic compounds (humus).

- Soil Horizons

  o As a result of these processes, soil will develop distinct layers, or horizons. **Soil horizons** are designated according to their soil profile position and the varying physical and chemical processes that created them.

  o Mature soil profiles usually include three basic master horizons: A, B, and C. There is also the O horizon (found above the A horizon and is comprised of organic material) and the E Horizon or eluvial horizon (found below the A horizon from which soluble materials have left).

    ✓ A horizon is often referred to as topsoil.

    ✓ B horizon is usually called subsoil.

    ✓ C horizon is sub-stratum.

  o Exposing and understanding the morphology of these horizons makes it possible to classify soil into types to predict structure and fertility.

Summary

Soil is formed by an ongoing, dynamic, and active process. Pedology is the study of soil formation, also known as pedogenesis and soil classification. All soil begins with solid rock. Wind, running water, rain, earthquakes, landslides, and other forces of nature, all play a role in the creation of soil. There are different types of weathering that occur: physical, chemical and biological. Though separate processes, they often work together to break down rock into the soil that is necessary for agricultural success. Rocks are classified into three broad types: igneous, sedimentary and metamorphic. The soil forming process involves the addition, loss, translocation or transformation of materials, and is governed by the five factors that influenced their formation: parent material, time, climate, organisms and topography. Because of these processes, soil horizons are created.

Additional Resources

Brady, N.C. and R. Weil. 2007. Nature and properties of soil. 14th ed. Englewood Cliffs, NJ: Prentice Hall.

Troeh, F.R. and L.M. Thompson. 2005. Soils and soil fertility. 6th ed. Ames, IA: Blackwell.

National Resources Conservation Service
http://www.nrcs.usda.gov/wps/portal/nrcs/main/national/soils/health/

Soil and Water Conservation Society
http://www.swcs.org/

Soil Science Society of America
https://www.soils.org/

Assessment

Take the online assessment here: https://goo.gl/BwcENv
Download and print the expanded written assessment by scanning this QR code or by going to this URL: https://www.tagmydoc.com/Ch02

Notes:

3 Soil Classification and Survey

Major Concept

Understanding the different soil classifications and how they can be used in soil surveys determines the best uses for soils.

Objectives

- Identify how soil surveys are prepared and used
- List three land capability classes and one characteristic of each
- List four things found in a soil report
- Identify the soil orders and one characteristic of each
- Define the difference between GPS and GIS
- Name four of the soil classification levels used for soil taxonomy

Key Terms

- Arable land
- Family
- Geographic Information System (GIS)
- Global Positioning Systems (GPS)
- Great group
- Land capability class
- Map units
- Order
- Series
- Soil classification
- Soil survey
- Subgroup
- Suborder
- Web Soil Survey

Chapter Resource

 Complementary *full color* illustrations, photos, charts and graphs are available by scanning this QR code or by following this URL https://www.tagmydoc.com/SS03 These digital resources will enhance your understanding of the chapter concepts.

Soil Classification

- **Soil Classification** is the process of arranging soil into categories based on common properties and according to usage.

- On a global level, several soil classification systems exist: Canadian System, Russian System, and Food and Agriculture Organization of the United Nations (FAO), are a few examples.

USDA

- The soil classification system presently used in the United States was developed by the United States Department of Agriculture (USDA) between 1951 and 1975. The system is called Soil Taxonomy (USDA Soil Survey Staff).

Soil Taxonomy

- Soil **taxonomy** is a system of classifying soils based on observable and quantifiable properties that can be viewed and sampled. Soils are grouped according to physical, chemical and mineralogical properties present in their soil horizons. This hierarchical system first places a soil in a broad category and then further narrows its category based on more detailed analysis.

- Soil taxonomy has six levels of classification from broadest to narrowest: **order, suborder, great group, subgroup, family** and **series:**

Classification Name	# in Group	Factors
Order	12	Based on presence or absence of key layers in the diagnostic horizon. The differences relate to dominant soil forming processes and degree of soil formation. Each order is identified by a word ending in 'sol.'
Suborder	66	Each of the above orders are divided into a suborder based on how they differ in wetness, climate, major parent material, vegetation and other factors.
Great Group	319	Each suborder is divided into great groups based on similar layers present in horizons with emphasis on presence or absence of specific diagnostic features, base status, soil temperature and soil moisture regimes. Named by adding prefix to suborder name.
Subgroup	2,484	Determined based on how the properties fit the typical concept of its great group. Describes characteristics such as wetness, sand, etc. New name is added before the great group name.
Family	8,000+	Families are established within a subgroup based on properties important to plant growth and soil uses such as texture, temperature, mineralogy and soil depth. Name composed of descriptive words placed before subgroup name.
Series	19,000+	Often named for a nearby town or landscape where first discovered. Consists of soils within a family that have similar color, texture, structure, reaction, mineral and chemical composition, and soil profile arrangement.

 Chapter Resource

Soil Orders

- 'Order' is the highest and most general of the soil classification system and is based on the conditions under which the soil developed. There are 12 soil orders. A helpful mnemonic to remember these soil orders is **I AM A SUAVE HOG**.

Order	Characteristics	% of world's ice-free land surface
Inceptisols *Slightly developed*	Immature soil with weakly developed subsurface horizons; Texture is finer than loamy very fine sand; Found throughout the world in semi-arid to humid environments	17%
Alfisols *Moderately weathered*	Moderately leached soils with subsurface zone of clay accumulation and greater than or equal to 35% base saturation; Formed in hardwood forests or under mixed vegetative cover; Fertile soil, productive for most crops	10%
Mollisols *Deep, fertile*	Dark, fertile grassland soils with high base saturation; Relatively high organic matter; Climates with moderate to pronounced seasonal moisture deficit	7%
Andisols *Volcanic ash*	Have minerals with unusually high water and nutrient-holding capacity; As a group, highly productive; Common in cool areas with moderate to high precipitation and/or areas with volcanic materials (ejecta)	1%
Spodosols *Sandy, acidic*	Acidic soils of coniferous pine forests of humid regions; Found in undisturbed areas; Tend to be infertile	4%
Ultisols *Weathered*	Forest soils of warm humid regions Low fertility, typically acidic soil, most nutrients in upper few inches; Lower capacity to retain additions of fertilizer, lime	8%
Aridisols *Very dry*	Desert soils, too dry for growth of plants that need adequate moisture; Lack of moisture limits development to upper part of the soils; Often accumulate gypsum, salt, calcium carbonate	12%
Vertisols *Swells and shrinks*	Crackling, dark clay soils that swell when wet Transmits water very slowly, very little leaching occurs; Tend to be high in natural fertility	2%
Entisols *Newly formed*	Primitive, developing soils; Found in areas of erosion or fast deposition rates such as dunes, slopes, and floodplains; Occur in many environments	16%
Histosols *Organic, wet*	High content of organic matter with no permafrost Commonly called bogs, moors, peats, or mucks Form in decomposed plant remains that accumulate in water, forest litter, or moss	1%
Oxisols *Very weathered*	Highly weathered soils found in tropical/subtropical regions; Tend to have indistinct horizons; Low natural fertility and low capacity to retain additions of fertilizer, lime	8%
Gelisols *Frozen*	Have permafrost near surface; May have evidence of frost churning and/or ice segregation Common in higher elevations	9%

Soil Survey

- **Soil survey** is the systematic examination, description, classification and mapping of soils in an area. Soil surveys are useful in understanding the suitability of soil for different uses (i.e.: crop production, livestock) and how soil behaves under various types of land management.

- Soil mapping (or field mapping) is the process of classifying soil types and geo-encoding the information. This is part of the soil survey process.

- A soil scientist will make predictions of soil type by factoring in the soil forming factors: climate, organism, relief, parent material and time. They will survey and measure slope, erosion and other features of the land.

- Aerial photographs and other useful information are accessed by soil scientists, usually on a computer tablet carried in the field.

- Predictions are verified by probing the soil and removing a core sample (using hand tools or hydraulic soil probe) where properties of the soil are observed and noted: depth to bedrock, abundance and distribution of roots, soil color and soil structure (texture, shape).

- Using GPS coordinates, exact locations are recorded and geo-encoded with the information.

Soil Survey Reports

- The USDA-Natural Resources Conservation Service (NRCS) Soil Survey Program produces a detailed Soil Survey Report based on the findings of the certified soil scientist.

- The U.S. Forest Service and the Bureau of Land Management conduct the surveys for the soils they have jurisdiction over.

- A soil survey report will generally consist of:

  o Four principal parts: (1) maps, (2) a map legend, (3) a description of the soils in the survey area, and (4) a use and management report.

  o Information tables regarding: temperature and precipitation, yields per acre of crops, range-land productivity, characteristic plant communities, windbreaks and environmental plantings, building site development, water management and classification of soils.

  o Predictions regarding soil behavior for selected land uses

  o Limitations and hazards inherent in the soil and improvements needed to overcome limitations

- Soil survey reports are helpful to many different land users:

Land Users	Reports Used For
Farmers, Ranchers, Foresters, Agronomists	Evaluate soil potential and needed management for maximum production
Planners, Engineers, Builders	Plan land use, select building sites, identify special treatment for foundation stability
Recreation, Wildlife Management, Conservationists	Understand potential need for environmental protection

Map Units

- A collection of areas defined and named the same in terms of their soil components and/or miscellaneous areas. It is an important part of visually understanding the soil survey.

- A soil survey will show the boundaries of mapping units with each unit being identified by codes and symbols that indicate different features.

- A map unit delineation on a map will be named according to the taxonomic classification (i.e.: soil series) of the dominant soil or miscellaneous area.

- Soil surveys use four kinds of map units to distinguish the different relationships: (1) consociations, (2) complexes, (3) associations, and (4) undifferentiated groups.

Advances in Technology

- **Global Positioning Systems (GPS)**

  o Allows instant identification of location with precise satellite coordinates.

  o Replaces need to estimate location using printed maps and identifiable landmarks.

- **Geographic Information System (GIS)**

  o Computerized data management system designed to capture, store, analyze, manage and display spatial and geographical information such as maps and reports.

  o Data is geo-referenced to the precise coordinates allowing for different data collections to be overlaid (to see relationships between different elements or note changes over time).

- **Web Soil Survey** (WSS)

  Chapter
  Resource

  o In the past, completed soil maps and accompanying information would be published in book form.

  o Soil survey results (and subsequent updates) are now published on the NRCS website, readily accessible to the public.

  o NRCS has soil maps and data available online for more than 95% of the nation's counties and anticipates having 100% soon.

  o "SoilWeb" is a new smart phone application available for users to instantly access soil survey information.

Land Capability Classes (I - VIII)

- Information from the soil survey indicates the soils' Land Capability Class.

- **Land Capability Classification** is a system of grouping soils on the basis of their "capability" to produce common cultivated crops and pasture plants without deteriorating over a long period of time.

  o Classes I-IV make up **arable land**, land suitable for crop production.

  o Classes V-VIII are non-arable land, not suitable for crop production but available for other uses.

- Following is an abbreviated version of the eight classes of the USDA Land Use Capability Classification System:

Suitable for Cultivation (Crop Production)	No Cultivation (Pasture, Hay, Woodland, and Wildlife)
I. Requires good soil management practices only ✓ Soils are deep, well drained, and land is nearly level	V. No restrictions in use ✓ Not likely to erode but have other limitations such as boulders and wetness which are impractical to correct
II. Moderate conservation practices necessary ✓ More limitations than Class I for intense crop production, such as moderately steep slopes	VI. Moderate restrictions in use ✓ Have greater need for good management due to steep slopes or shallow soils
III. Intensive conservation practices necessary ✓ Shallow soils and steep slopes	VII. Severe restriction in use ✓ Use restricted to grazing, woodland or wildlife
IV. Perennial vegetation, infrequent cultivation ✓ Most of the time should be in "permanent" crops (such as pastures)	VIII. Best suited for wildlife and recreation ✓ Severely limited due to steep slopes, rocklands or swamps

- Land Capability Subclass is the second category in the land capability classification system.

    - Class codes e, w, s, and c are used for land capability subclasses and indicate what the soil use limitations are

Land Capability Subclass	Soil Use Limitations
Subclass e	Soils susceptible to erosion or have had past erosion damage, runoff issues, slopes greater than 2%
Subclass w	Soils use limited due to excess water, poor drainage, wetness and overflow issues
Subclass s	Soils with rooting zone limitations due to shallowness, stones, low moisture-holding capacity, low fertility that is difficult to correct and salinity or sodium content.
Subclass c	Soils where climate is a hazard or issue, temperature extremes, lack of rainfall

Summary

Soil is somewhat predictable. Once it is categorized, a soil based on its known properties, predictions can be made for how the soil will behave. A soil classification system is a comprehensive way to record a soil's classification or "name" in order that land users can make informed decisions on how to best utilize, manage or manipulate a particular section of land based on those predictors. Soil Taxonomy is a system developed in the United States and utilizes six levels of classification (using a hierarchical method): soil order, suborders, great groups, subgroups, families and soil series. Soil order, the broadest group, has 12 classifications. Soil series, the most defined level, has over 19,000 soil classifications. Soil surveys, mapping and survey reports, provide information such as: maps and legends, land capability class, soil properties and land use and management advice. This information is invaluable, not just to farmers and ranchers, but to engineers, builders, recreation and wildlife managers and more. Methods of surveying and classifying soil have made huge advancements. Results once published in hard copy books have been replaced with web access, GPS, GIS, and even smart phone 'apps' that provide instant and customized reports. In the field of agriculture, soil classification and surveys are crucial to determining key factors towards success. For example, this information can tell a grower what crops will do well on a certain section of land or what fertilizers may need to be added to the soil. These processes look at a soil's past to predict its future.

Additional Resources

Ashman, M.R. and G. Puri. 2002. Essential soil science. Ames, IA: Blackwell Publishing.

Plaster, E.J. 2013. Soil science and management. 6th Ed. Clifton Park, NY: Delmar, Cengage Learning.

Soil and Water Conservation Society
http://www.swcs.org/

Soil Science Society of America
https://www.soils.org/

National Resources Conservation Service
http://www.nrcs.usda.gov/wps/portal/nrcs/main/national/soils/health/

Assessment

 Take the online assessment here: https://goo.gl/BY8BxB
Download and print the expanded written assessment by scanning this QR
code or by going to this URL: https://www.tagmydoc.com/Ch03

Notes:

4 Physical Properties of Soil

Major Concept

Physical properties of soil are the composition, texture, structure, bulk density, depth, color and water-holding capacities.

Objectives

- List two soil definitions
- Name the four substances of soil
- Define the use of a soil texture triangle
- List the three major classes of soil structure
- Name the two primary colors of soil
- Define the range of water available to plants
- List the three main parts of a soil profile
- Identify the chemical properties of soil
- Name four ways organic matter benefits the soil
- List three ways soils are classified

Key Terms

- Acidic
- Aggregates
- Alkaline
- Buffering
- Bulk density
- Cation exchange capacity(CEC)
- Field capacity (FC)
- Hygroscopic water

- Immobilization
- Mineralization
- Neutral
- Organic matter
- Parent material
- Permanent wilting point (PWP)
- pH
- Pore space

- Saline
- Sodic
- Soil classification
- Soil texture
- Soil texture triangle
- Structure
- Subsoil
- Topsoil

Chapter Resource

Complementary *full color* illustrations, photos, charts and graphs are available by scanning this QR code or by following this URL: https://www.tagmydoc.com/SS04 These digital resources will enhance your understanding of the chapter concepts.

Soil Definitions

- Material which nourishes and supports growing plants, including rocks, water, snow and even air – all of which can support plant life.

- Geologically, defined as the loose surface of the earth as distinguished from solid bedrock. A mixture of mineral matter, organic matter, water and air.

  - Soil taxonomy defines soil as a collection of natural bodies of the earth's surface, in places modified or even made by man or earthy materials, containing living matter and supporting or capable of supporting plants out-of-doors.

    - ✓ Upper limit is air or shallow water.

    - ✓ Extremes run from deep water to barren areas of rock or ice.

    - ✓ Lower limit is the lower limit of biologic activity, which generally coincides with the common rooting depth of native perennial plants.

Physical Properties

- Include: composition, texture, structure, bulk density, depth, color and water-holding capacity.

  - Consists of four substances:

    1. Small mineral particles from the breakdown of rocks.

    2. **Organic matter** is plant and animal material, both dead and living.

    3. Water

    4. Air

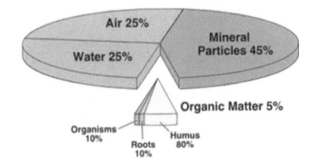

  - Microbes break down wastes and dead plant and animal material, and convert it into forms which can be used as food by living plants.

  - Other soil microbes take nitrogen gas from the air and convert it into forms which plants can use as food.

- **Soil Texture**

  - Refers to the amount of sand, silt and clay in the soil.

    - ✓ Best understood by rubbing samples of moist soil between thumb and finger.

- ✓ Sand particles are largest in size and can be seen with the naked eye and feel gritty between thumb and finger.

- ✓ Silt is intermediate in size between sand and clay and also intermediate in many other ways between sand and clay. These particles are too small to be seen by the eye, but are visible under a microscope. Silt feels smooth, like talcum powder.

- ✓ Clay is the smallest particle and usually feels slick and sticky when wet, firm when moist and hard when dry.

  o Combinations of sand, silt and clay are usually described as follows:

  - ✓ **Fine Texture** -Soils made up of mostly clay particles.

  - ✓ **Medium Texture** - Soils are silty or loamy in nature. To the touch, feel should be between fine and coarse texture.

  - ✓ **Coarse Texture** - Soils which have a high content of sand and feel similar to table salt.

  o Soil texture determines amount and size of spaces between soil particles which determines water movement and amount of water soil will hold.

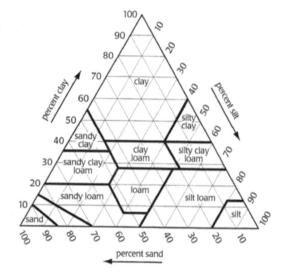

- • **Soil Texture Triangle**

  o Used to determine textural name of a soil by measuring percentage of sand, silt and clay present in soil.

  o After percentages of silt and clay are determined, these amounts are plotted on the soil triangle.

Soil Structure

- • **Structure** refers to the arrangement of soil particles. A well-developed structure usually indicates the presence of clay.

  o Classified into three major classes and several sub-classes:

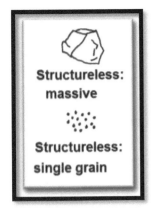

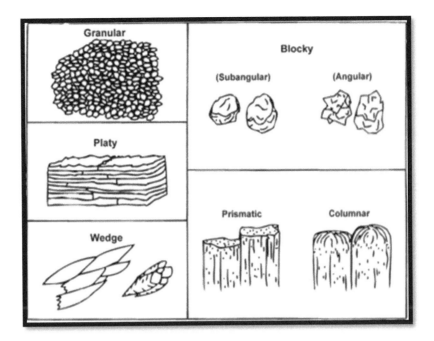

1. Structureless which includes single grain and massive.

2. With-structure class includes granular, platy, wedge, blocky, prismatic and columnar.

3. Structure-destroyed class includes puddle.

- Soil structure is particularly important in the absorption of water and circulation of air.

  - Three very important aspects of soil structure include:

    1. Arrangement into aggregates of a desirable shape and size.

    2. Stability of the **aggregate** (groups of soil particles that bind to each other more strongly than to adjacent particles).

    3. The space between the aggregates provides pore space for retention and exchange of air and water; whether or not they are connected by channels or isolated.

  - Aggregates stable in water permit a greater rate of absorption of water and greater resistance to erosion. Aggregates unstable in water tend to slake and disperse.

  - When exposed to raindrops, aggregates are particularly subject to dispersion and the resultant crusting of soils.

    ✓ Crusting greatly affects seedling emergence and increases runoff and erosion.

- Stability of aggregates is due to:

  ✓ Type of clay

  ✓ Chemical elements associated with the clay

  ✓ Nature of the products of decomposition or organic matter

  ✓ Nature of microbial population

- Other factors affecting soil and known to improve soil structure:

  ✓ Freezing and thawing

  ✓ Wetting and drying

  ✓ Action of burrowing insects and animals

  ✓ Growth of root systems of plants

Chapter
Resource

- All of these have a loosening effect on the soil, but no part in aggregate stability.

- Loosening of the soil is a necessary part of aggregate formation, not aggregate stability.

- **Bulk Density**

  - Refers to the weight of the oven–dry (moisture removed) soil with its natural structural arrangement.

  - **Pore space** is a part of the volume of soil measured for bulk density.

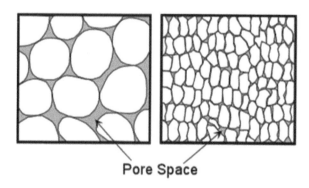

Pore Space

  - Bulk density = weight of oven-dry soil in grams (g) divided by its volume in cubic centimeters (cc).

  - Any variation in bulk density is due largely to the difference in total pore space.

- ✓ Finer textured soils have higher percentages of total pore space therefore finer textured soils have smaller bulk density values.

- ✓ High and low bulk densities have great influences on engineering properties, water movement, rooting depth of plants and many other physical attributes for soil interpretations.

- Soil Depth

  - ○ Total depth of topsoil, subsoil and parent material which will allow growth of plant roots.

  - ○ Depth of soil can cause the yield of a crop to be high or low. Deeply rooted plants, such as alfalfa, will not grow well when planted in a shallow soil.

  - ○ **Soil depth** is the distance between the soil surface and the layer which is unfavorable for root growth.

- Soil Colors

  - ○ Important feature in recognizing different soil types, but also indicates certain physical and chemical characteristics.

  - ○ Primary factors in soil color

    - ✓ Humus content (**organic matter**)

    - ✓ Chemical nature of the iron compounds present in the soil.

  - ○ Very high content of humus may mask the color of the mineral matter to such an extent that the soil appears almost black regardless of the color status of the iron compounds.

  - ○ Iron is an important color material because iron appears as a stain on the surfaces of mineral particles.

    - ✓ About 5% or more of mineral soils is iron.

    - ✓ In un-weathered soils iron has little or no influence on color.

    - ✓ Iron that has the greatest effect on color is weathered from primary minerals and exits in the oxide or hydroxide form.

Water Relations

- Size, shape and arrangement of the soil particles and the associated voids (pores) determine the ability of a soil to retain water.

  - Large pores in the soil can conduct more water more rapidly than fine pores.

    - ✓ Removing water from large pores is easier and requires less energy than removing water from smaller pores.

  - Sandy soils consist mainly of large mineral particles with very small percentages of clay, silt and organic matter.

    - ✓ Sandy soils have many more large pores than clayey soils.

    - ✓ Total volume of pores in sandy soils is significantly smaller than in clayey soils (30 to 40% for sandy soils as compared to 40 to 60% for clayey soils).

    - ✓ A significant number of the pores in sandy soils are large enough to drain within the first 24 hours due to gravity and this portion of water is lost from the system before plants can use it.

- Plant Water

  - To study soil-water-plant relationships, subdivide soil water into:

    - ✓ Water available to the plant

    - ✓ Water unavailable to the plant

  - Most **gravitational water** moves out of the root zone too rapidly to be used by the plants.

  - Remaining water stored under tension in the various size pores.

  - The smaller the pore the greater the tension and the more energy required to remove its water.

    - ✓ Removal of water from very small pores requires too much energy and consequently, this water is not available to the plant.

    - ✓ Some water very closely bound to soil particles called **hygroscopic water**, is very difficult to remove, and is not available to the plants.

  - The range of water available to plants is between field capacity (FC) and the permanent wilting point (PWP).

✓ Soil is at **field capacity (FC)** when all the gravitational water has been drained and a vertical movement of water due to gravity is negligible.

✓ **Permanent Wilting Point (PWP)** is defined as the point where no more water is available to the plant.

Soil Profile

- Arrangement and properties of the various soil layers; namely: topsoil, subsoil and parent material; horizons vary from soil to soil in thickness, texture, color and other properties.

    o **Topsoil** is the surface or very top layer of soil.

    ✓ Usually called A Horizon

    ✓ Ranges from a depth of a few inches to several feet

    ✓ Darker than other layers because it contains organic matter

    ✓ Usually softer and more easily worked than the underlying areas

    ✓ **Subsoil** is the layer just under the topsoil

    ✓ Usually called B Horizon and may be higher in clay content

    ✓ May be red, brown, yellow or gray in color

    ✓ Usually lighter in color, since little or no organic matter is present

    ✓ Usually firmer and more difficult to penetrate than topsoil

    o **Parent material** is the lowest layer.

    ✓ May be the C Horizon from which topsoil and subsoil have developed (A and B Horizons).

    ✓ May be firm and difficult for roots to penetrate, or may be soft enough to allow root growth.

    ✓ Solid rock may exist under C horizon.

    ✓ C horizon may form from rock, or may form in loose material (sand, silt, clay or gravel) put in place by water, gravity, glaciers or wind.

Chemical Properties

- Includes: **pH** (acidity or alkalinity), **cation exchange capacity** (total number of exchangeable cations a soil can adsorb), sodic, saline and organic matter.

  o These relate to plant growth and availability of nutrients.

- Soil pH

  o Soil's water contains dissolved mineral salts known as the **soil solution** (liquid phase of soil consists of water and dissolved ions). The way the soil solution reacts determines the acidity, alkalinity (basic) or neutrality of the soil.

  o Some soil contains more hydrogen ions (H^+) than hydroxyl ions (OH^-). This makes them **acidic**.

  o Other soils contain more hydroxyl ions than hydrogen ions. They are termed **alkaline** (basic).

  o When a soil contains equal concentrations of hydrogen and hydroxyl ions, it is termed **neutral soil**.

  o Exact relationship between the hydrogen and hydroxyl ions is expressed as a pH number.

    ✓ 7.0 is neutral; less than 7.0 is acidic; more than 7.0 is alkaline (basic)

    ✓ pH of a soil can only be measured precisely using an instrument known as a pH meter

    ✓ Additions to the soil that increase the number of H+ ions will lower the pH of the soil while soil additions that increase the number of OH- ions will raise the soil pH.

    ✓ Many of the materials used to improve the structure and texture of the soil will also modify its pH:

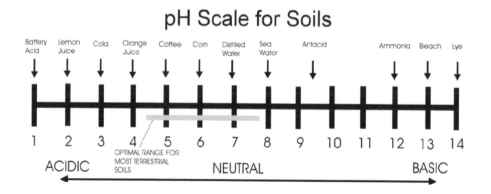

pH Scale for Soils

- ✓ Peat moss is highly acidic, and its addition to the soil as a source of organic material will have a direct impact on the acidity of the soil solution

- ✓ Limestone has the opposite effect, contributing alkalinity to the solution.

- o **Buffering** occurs when the soil solution contains either a weak acid and its salt or a weak base and its salt, which is resistant to changes in pH.

  - ✓ These substances prevent a rapid change in pH when acids or alkalis are added to the soil.

  - ✓ Includes clay, humus and carbonates.

- o Within the pH range of 4.0 to 9.0, the availability of many mineral nutrients is determined by the acidity or alkalinity of the soil.

  - ✓ For example, some plants will exhibit a distinctly patterned yellowing or chlorosis, when grown in soil having a high pH.

- o Cause of the chlorosis is lack of iron in the plant tissue, and it results because iron compounds, needed by the plant, are precipitated out of the soil solution and rendered unavailable to the plants.

Chapter Resource

- • **Cation Exchange Capacity (CEC)**

  - o For more details refer to Topic 10: Soil Fertility

  - o Total number of exchangeable cations a soil can hold (the amount of its negative charge) is called its cation exchange capacity or CEC. This means they are exchangeable.

  - o Calcium (C) can be exchanged for $H+$ and/or $K+$ (potassium ions) and vice versa. Generally, cations with higher numbers of charges (higher charge density) are more tightly held (absorbed) by colloids.

    - ✓ Those cations can be exchanged or replaced by large numbers of cations with lower charge density (mass action).

    - ✓ The higher a soil's CEC, the more cations it can retain. Soils differ in their capacities to hold exchangeable $K+$ and other cations.

    - ✓ CEC depends on amounts and kinds of clay and organic matter present. CEC increases as organic matter increases.

- Expressing CEC

  - CEC of a soil expressed in terms of milligram equivalents per 100 grams of soil and written as meq/100 g.

    - ✓ Clay minerals usually range from 10 to 150 meq/100 g in CEC values.

    - ✓ Organic matter ranges from 200 to 400 meq/100 g.

    - ✓ Kind and amount of clay and organic matter content greatly influence the CEC of soils.

- Using the CEC

  - Where soils are highly weathered and organic matter levels are low, CEC values are low.

  - Where less weathering occurred, and organic matter levels are usually higher, CEC values can be quite high.

  - Clay soils with high CEC can retain large amounts of cations against potential loss by leaching.

  - Sandy soils with low CEC retain smaller quantities of cations.

- Sodic and Saline Soils

  - **Sodic** or alkali soils contain excessive amounts of sodium (Na) on the soil CEC sites.

    - ✓ Usually classified as sodic if sodium (Na) saturation exceeds 15% of the CEC.

    - ✓ pH values usually 8.5 and above.

    - ✓ Excess sodium (Na) disperses in the soil, limiting the movement of air and water because of poor physical properties.

    - ✓ Water tends to pond on sodic soils.

  - Such soils can be reclaimed by replacing the sodium (Na) on the CEC complex with calcium (Ca).

    - ✓ Gypsum (calcium sulfate) is the most common treatment but elemental sulfur (S) can be used if the soil is calcareous.

    - ✓ Successful reclamation requires sodium (Na) to be leached out of root zone.

- ✓ Deep ripping and/or manure application has been used to improve internal water movement

- Saline-Sodic Soils

  - Sometimes sodic soils will also be **saline** (salty).

    - ✓ Typically characterized by sodium (Na) saturation greater than 15% of the CEC and a pH of 8.4 or less.

  - Reclamation is the same as that for sodic soils.

Organic Matter

- Consists of plant and animal residues in various stages of decay. Adequate levels benefit soil in four ways:

  1. Improves physical condition and structure

  2. Increases water infiltration

  3. Decreases erosion losses

  4. Supplies plant nutrients

Chapter
Resource

- Release of Nitrogen (N)

  - Organic matter serves as a storehouse for Nitrogen (N) but decays slowly so is not readily available for plants.

  - Other nutrients such as magnesium (Mg), calcium (Ca), sulfur (S) and micronutrients are also contained in organic matter.

    - ✓ As decomposition occurs, these become available to growing plants.

    - ✓ Some nutrients such as nitrogen (N) and sulfur (S) can be temporarily tied up during the process.

    - ✓ If the organic matter being decomposed has a high carbon to nitrogen (C:N) ratio, meaning low nitrogen (N), microorganisms will use available soil and fertilizer nitrogen (N), a process called **immobilization**.

    - ✓ Eventually nitrogen (N) immobilized into the bodies of soil organisms become available as the organisms die and decay. This is called **mineralization**.

- Variability

  - In tropical areas, most soils are inherently low in organic matter because warm temperatures and high rainfall increase decomposition.

  - In cooler areas, where decomposition takes place more slowly, native organic matter levels can be quite high.

    - ✓ With adequate fertilization and good management practices crop residues are produced and added to soil, maintaining or increasing organic matter levels in soils.

Scientific Soil Classification

- Soils have been classified for hundreds of years.

  - Soils have been grouped according to:

    - ✓ Agronomic use - good wheat soil, poor corn soil, etc.

    - ✓ Color - black soil, red soil, etc.,

    - ✓ Organic matter content - mineral soil, muck soil, peat soil, etc.

    - ✓ **Texture** - sand, sandy loam, loam, etc.

    - ✓ Moisture condition - wet soil, dry soil, etc.

  - A new system of soil classification was adopted for use in the United States on January 1, 1965.

    - ✓ Treats soils as individual three-dimensional entities which can be grouped together according to their similar physical, chemical and mineralogical properties.

    - ✓ Consists of 12 soil orders based on broad differences in measurable and visible characteristics of certain kinds of soil horizons. The soil orders are: Entisols, Mollisols, Vertisols, Inceptisols, Aridisols, Spodosols, Alfisols, Ultisols, Oxisols and Histosols.

  - Each of the orders is divided into several suborders. (Refer to Topic 3: Soil Classification and Survey

- Simple Classification of Land

  - Useful to people who are buying or selling land; such as: excellent, good or poor for a certain crop; irrigated or non-irrigated; or the dollar value per acre.

- Practical Classifications of Land

  o Several practical land classification systems are presently in use. For example:

    ✓ Agronomists may classify land on the ability of soils to grow the common field crops.

    ✓ Foresters may classify land according to the rate of tree growth, using good, fair, poor, and so on, as land classes.

  o Developed by the Soil Conservation Service one of the most widely used land classification systems divides all lands into eight capability classes, based on the capability of land, degree of erosion, etc. The eight classifications are:

    1. Class I – Few limitations for cultivated agriculture

    2. Class II – Suitable for all uses with mild limitations

    3. Class III – Grow the same crops as I and II - Serious problems needing consideration

    4. Class IV – Marginal for cultivated crops – Limitations same as Class III but more severe

    5. Class V – Not suited to cultivated crops — Limited by flooding, short growing season, rocks, wetlands

    6. Class VI – Not suitable to cultivated crops — Limited by steep slopes, erosion, drought

    7. Class VII – Same problems as Class VI but more severe

    8. Class VIII – Cannot support any commercial plant production

Summary

Various definitions apply to soils. The physical and chemical properties of soils influence their ability to grow plants. Physical properties of soil include composition, texture, structure, bulk density, depth, color, and water-holding capacity. Chemical properties of soils include pH, cation exchange capacity, sodic, saline, and organic matter. Soils are classified according to the percent of sand, silt, or clay they contain. Soils are very different in their ability to provide nutrients. Soil also provides plants with water. Soil pH, cation exchange capability, organic matter, and drainage are factors that influence the ability of a soil to grow a crop. Soil is classified into 12 categories. Soil is also divided into eight land capability classes.

Additional Resources

Brady, N.C. and R. Weil. 2007. Nature and properties of soil. 14th ed. Englewood Cliffs, NJ: Prentice Hall.

Parker, R. 2010. Plant and soil science. Clifton Park, NY: Delmar Publishing.

United States Department of Agriculture. 1957. Soil: The yearbook of agriculture. Washington, D.C.: United States Government Printing Office.

Soil and Water Conservation Society
http://www.swcs.org/

Soil Science Society of America
https://www.soils.org/

National Resources Conservation Service
http://www.nrcs.usda.gov//

Assessment

Take the online assessment here: https://goo.gl/7LguU4
Download and print the expanded written assessment by scanning this QR code or by going to this URL: https://www.tagmydoc.com/Ch04

Notes:

5 Soil Life

Major Concept

The activity that occurs in and interacts with the soil begins with the organisms and includes nutrients, plants and soil animals.

Objectives

- Define the food web
- Outline the carbon cycle and explain its importance
- Identify soil organisms and list ways they are important
- List the four classifications of soil organisms and give examples of each
- Name the three main forms of microflora and give one function of each
- List and explain three functions of microorganisms
- Describe three ways to encourage beneficial soil organisms
- Explain the three main parts of the nitrogen cycle
- Identify two ways animals affect soil

Key Terms

- Actinomycete
- Algae
- Arthropod
- Autotroph
- Denitrification
- Fungi
- Heterotroph
- Immobilization
- Inoculation
- Macrofauna
- Mesofauna
- Microfauna
- Microflora
- Mineralization
- Mycorrhizae
- Nematode
- Nitrification
- Nitrogen fixation
- Primary consumer
- Primary producer
- Saprophyte
- Secondary consumers
- Symbiont

Chapter Resource

Complementary *full color* illustrations, photos, charts and graphs are available by scanning this QR code or by following this URL: https://www.tagmydoc.com/SS05 These digital resources will enhance your understanding of the chapter concepts.

Soil Food Web

- Soil is home to a living ecosystem. The soil food web is made up of the community of organisms that live in or visit the soil. While a food chain describes one direct pathway through an ecosystem, a food web is more complex, and it shows the many potential interactions occurring between organisms.

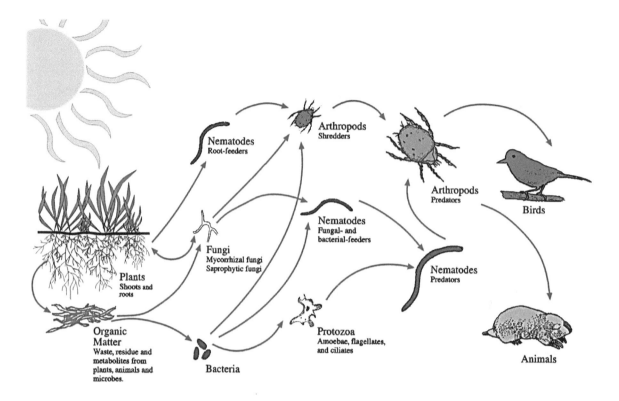

- Biological Carbon Cycle

  - Soil, an important part of the biological carbon cycle, is a significant source of carbon. The carbon cycle begins in plants, which combine carbon dioxide from the atmosphere with water to make plant tissues. Animals that eat the plants later die. Their decaying tissue is eaten by soil organisms, a process that releases carbon dioxide.

    - ✓ In one part of the biological carbon cycle, plants remove carbon dioxide (CO_2) from the atmosphere by the process of photosynthesis.

    - ✓ This process results in inorganic compounds being converted to organic carbon which is a major component of soil organic matter.

    - ✓ Soil microorganisms like algae, lichens, and photosynthetic bacteria are important in the sequestration of carbon in the soil.

    - ✓ In the soil, there are two major types of soil carbon. Biomass, which is the living bacteria and fungi, and non-biomass carbon, which is the cellulose, starch, and lignin in dead plants.

  - As the soil food web decomposes organic material, it releases carbon into the atmosphere as CO_2 or converts it to a variety of forms of soil organic matter.

- Decomposition

  o Decomposition of living and dead organic matter results in necessary nutrients for plants and other soil organisms.

    ✓ Decomposition, one of the steps to energy transformation, is an important part of the soil food web.

    ✓ Plant nutrients from decayed plants and animals are released resulting in carbon in the soil.

Soil Organisms

- Soil is teeming with life, from that which is visible, like an earthworm; to the tiniest microorganisms only seen with a microscope, like protozoa. These soil organisms vary in size, complexity and characteristics and can be categorized many ways.

  o Ecological Function: One way to categorize soil organisms. All ecosystems have producers and consumers in the food chain.

  o Trophic Levels: The trophic level of an organism is the position it holds in the food chain (or food web).

  o **Primary producers**, or **autotrophs**, are organisms (for example: plants) that produce their own food. They are the base of the food chain.

  o **Heterotrophs** are the consumers in food chains. They cannot make their own food and get their energy from eating autotrophs or other heterotrophs.

    ✓ **Primary consumers** eat the primary producers.

    ✓ **Secondary consumers** consume the primary consumers.

    ✓ Heterotrophs break down complex organic compounds into simpler compounds, release energy by oxidizing carbon and hydrogen atoms, producing carbon dioxide and water.

Chapter Resource

    ✓ Examples of Heterotrophs:

      ▪ Parasites - Feed on plant roots, often responsible for plant diseases.

      ▪ Predators - Prey on other soil life, keep parasite populations in check and perform other functions.

      ▪ **Saprophytes** - Decomposers, feed on dead organic matter.

> **Symbionts** - Organisms that live with another organism in a partnership or 'symbiotic' relationship (beneficial to both).

- Soil organisms can be grouped according to their preferred environment.

  o Aerobic: Organisms that require oxygen to live and grow are called aerobic.

    ✓ Aerobic organisms do best in a soil that is moist but not flooded or saturated as this would deprive them of the oxygen they need.

    ✓ They also will do well with a neutral soil pH and plenty of food or organic matter available.

  o Anaerobic: Organisms that do not require oxygen are called anaerobic.

    ✓ Anaerobic organisms can live in flooded and saturated soils as they do not require oxygen.

    ✓ Microbial communities in anaerobic soils play a key role in regulating cycles and releasing nutrients back into the environment.

Size and Taxonomy of Soil Organisms

- A common classification method of soil organisms is according to taxonomy and size, separating soil organisms into macrofauna, mesofauna, microfauna and microflora.

Classification	Body Width	Examples
Macrofauna	>2mm	Snails, Slugs, Earthworms, Ants, Termites, Millipedes, Woodlice
Mesofauna	0.1 to 2 mm	Arthropods: Mites, Collembola, Enchytraeids, Nematodes*
Microfauna	<0.1 mm	Protozoa
Microflora (microorganisms)	<100 μm	Bacteria, Actinomycetes, Fungi, Viruses, Algae

*Nematodes and microarthropods are sometimes placed in the microfauna category.

- Macrofauna

  o Because of their feeding and burrowing activities, soil **macrofauna** assist in regulating decomposition, nutrient cycling, and creating water pathways. One important macrofauna member is the earthworm.

  o Earthworms are invertebrates and hermaphrodites (both male and female characteristics). There are more than 7,000 species of earthworms.

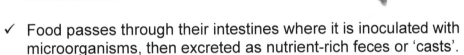

✓ Between 200 and 1,000 lbs. of earthworms may occupy an acre of soil.

✓ Presence of earthworms is usually a sign of a healthy soil system.

✓ They feed on organic matter and its fungi and bacteria.

✓ Food passes through their intestines where it is inoculated with microorganisms, then excreted as nutrient-rich feces or 'casts'.

✓ The increased microbial activity that occurs helps to facilitate conversion of nutrients to be readily used by plants.

✓ As earthworm's burrow, they aerate the soil, minimize surface water erosion, and provide nutrient rich channels for plant roots to grow.

✓ Different species of earthworms live in different parts of the soil. They can be classified into three ecological groups based on their mode of living.

o Earthworm Groups:

Species	Location	Habits
Epigeic	Surface soil	■ Live in or near surface plant litter ■ Small, adapted to ever changing moisture levels and temperature of the surface
Endogeic	Shallow soil	■ Feed on soil and organic matter ■ Utilize temporary channels that become filled with their cast material as they move through the soil
Anecic	Deep soil	■ Have permanent burrow system ■ Feed mostly on surface plant litter which they pull into their tunnels (up to several meters deep) ■ May leave plugs blocking the burrow opening

- **Mesofauna** typically live within soil pores, have limited burrowing ability (mostly inhabit surface litter) and feed on organic materials, microflora, microfauna and other invertebrates. Some examples of mesofauna organisms are:

  o **Arthropods**

    ✓ Arthropods include insects, such as springtails, beetles and ants; crustaceans such as sowbugs; arachnids such as spiders and mites; myriapods, such as centipedes and millipedes; and scorpions.

✓ Arthropods are invertebrates (no backbone, exoskeleton) and have jointed legs: 'Arthros' means jointed and 'podos' means legs.

✓ Arthropods can be grouped as shredders, predators, herbivores, and fungal-feeders, based on their functions in soil:

- Shredders: Chew up dead plant matter, eat bacteria and fungi on plant matter surface. Examples of shredders are: millipedes, sowbugs, termites, certain mites and roaches. Can become a pest if feed on live roots (when sufficient dead plant material is not present).

- Predators: Many predators, such as centipedes, spiders, scorpions, pseudoscorpions and ants eat crop pests. Some predators (for example: beetles and parasitic wasps) are used as commercial biocontrols.

- Herbivores: Cicadas, mole-crickets and anthomyiid flies feed on roots and live all or part of their life underground. Some herbivores, for example the symphylan and the rootworm, can become an agricultural problem when they occur in large numbers as they feed on roots or other plant parts.

- Fungal Feeders: Include most springtails, silverfish and some mites. They scrape and consume fungi and bacteria from root surfaces. They provide a large part of nutrients available to plants.

- Collembola or "springtails": Springtails are notable as they are one of the main biological agents responsible for the control and dissemination of soil microorganisms. They are beneficial to crop plants because they release nutrients and feed on diseases caused by fungi.

o Nematodes

✓ **Nematodes** are a diverse group of non-segmented worms under 1 mm long. They are often categorized according to their diet.

✓ While some nematodes cause disease and are a crop pest because they feed on plant roots, other nematodes actually consume disease-causing organisms.

✓ Nematodes release nutrients for plants and distribute bacteria and fungi through the soil.

Nematode Type	Diet	Habits
Bacterial-feeders	Bacteria	Mouthpart is a hollow tube that sucks in bacteria
Fungal-feeders	Fungi	Puncture the cell wall of fungi and sucking out inside contents
Predatory	Other Nematodes, Protozoa	Eat smaller organisms whole or attach to larger nematode scraping away until internal body parts are extracted
Omnivores	Variety of organisms	May have a different diet at different life stages
Root-feeders	Plant roots	Plant parasite; do not live in the soil

- **Microfauna** are the smallest of soil organisms and have to be viewed with a microscope. The most important of the microfauna is the protozoa.

  o Protozoa – Protozoa are tiny, single celled animals that vary in shape and include amoebas, ciliates and flagellates.

  o They are major consumers of bacteria, thereby regulating bacterial population. They also feed on soil particles and roots.

  o Their flexibility allows them to slide over surfaces and to feed within thin water films around soil particles.

  o As they feed on bacteria, they release excess nitrogen which is used by the food web.

  o They are a food source for other soil organisms and help to suppress disease by feeding on pathogens or competing with pathogens.

Microflora (microorganisms)

- There are three main forms of **microflora** in soils: bacteria, fungi and viruses. Also included in this category are algae and actinomycetes.

  o Bacteria – single-celled organism responsible for soil breakdown

    ✓ Able to multiply; can adjust their population quickly in response to environmental changes.

    ✓ Aerobic and anaerobic.

    ✓ Enzymes break down simple compounds, such as sugar and cellulose.

    ✓ Responsible for several important enzymatic transformations:

      ▪ Nitrogen oxidation

- Sulfur oxidation

- Nitrogen fixation

- **Fungi** – more complex, non-photosynthetic, multi-celled organisms (except yeast, which is single celled)

  ✓ Live on dead or living plant or animal tissue.

  ✓ Fungi hasten nutrient cycling.

  ✓ Vigorous decomposers of organic matter and readily attack cellulose, lignins and other complex compounds.

  ✓ Secrete substances that aid in formation of soil aggregates.

  ✓ Continue the decomposition process after bacteria and actinomycetes have essentially ceased to function.

  ✓ Some fungi can cause root rot in seedlings and fungus in potatoes; many fungi are plant parasites.

  ✓ **Mycorrhizae** are fungi that form a symbiotic (mutually beneficial) relationship with plant roots and help with plant growth.

    - This fungi aid in transmitting nutrients and water to the plant roots.

    - Increases plant seedlings tolerance to drought and high temperature and resistance to infection from diseased fungi.

    - It is thought mycorrhizae cause plant roots to absorb extra nutrients due to the additional absorbing surface provided by the fungi (up to ten times greater).

- Viruses – smallest, simplest, multiplying entity; parasite

  ✓ All are parasites: live off other flora or fauna.

  ✓ Numbers impacted by moisture, surface of soil aggregates, rooting system and structural units of plants.

✓ Little is known about viruses in the soil. Their importance is still being discovered.

o **Algae** – microscopic, chlorophyll-bearing organisms

   ✓ Can produce new photosynthetic growth

   ✓ Single-celled, can photosynthesize; considered primary producers.

   ✓ Some symbiotic algae associate with one of several fungi in forms called 'lichens'.

   ✓ Under the right conditions of moisture and light will produce considerable amount of organic material.

o **Actinomycetes** – group of organisms with characteristics between bacteria and fungi (often called mold bacteria)

   ✓ Decompose cellulose and other resistant organic matter.

   ✓ Secrete non-water soluble gummy substance which aids in formation of desirable soil structure.

   ✓ Form symbiotic nitrogen fixing relationships with many plant families.

   ✓ Produce many useful antibiotics including streptomycin, auremycin, terramycin and neomycin.

   ✓ Can work in dry, alkaline or high temperature soils.

   ✓ Produce chemicals that stop microorganism growth.

   ✓ Can protect some plant roots from disease.

• Microorganisms live mostly in the top two feet of soil which includes air, water and food to thrive; other organic chemicals are leaked from plant roots into the surrounding soil which are beneficial to microorganisms.

Functions of Microorganisms

• Nutrient Cycling

   o The movement of nutrients from the physical environment into plants and animals and back again is called the nutrient cycle.

- Nitrogen (N), phosphorus (P), potassium (K), calcium (Ca), magnesium (Mg), sulfur (S), iron (Fe), manganese (Mn), zinc (Zn), copper (Cu), boron (B), molybdenum (Mo) and chlorine (Cl) are obtained from the soil and required by all plants.

- **Immobilization**: Micro-organisms absorb nutrients released from organic matter decomposition, preventing these nutrients from being available to plants. The opposite to mineralization.

- **Mineralization**: Microbial decomposers change immobilized nutrients into an inorganic substance, so plants can use them.

- Plants cannot use immobilized nutrients until they have been changed to an inorganic substance.

- Nutrient Immobilization

  - Mineral nutrients are incorporated into microbial biomass.

  - Nutrients in fresh organic matter are bound in complex organic forms.

  - Sulfur cycle: Opposite of immobilization and mineralization.

    ✓ Soil organisms participate in the sulfur cycle by breaking up the abundant sulfur compounds making this element available to plants.

    ✓ Plants absorb sulfate to make protein and other compounds, immobilizing the sulfur.

    ✓ Some sulfate is taken up by plants, some is again immobilized in the bodies of microorganisms, and some leaches away.

    ✓ The rotten egg smell found in swamps and marshes is from the hydrogen sulfide produced by microorganisms.

- Nitrogen Cycle

  - **Nitrogen Fixation** is part of the nitrogen cycle. Before nitrogen can be used by plants, it must first be removed from the atmosphere – either naturally through nitrogen fixation, which occurs in green plants called legumes or commercially through fertilizer plants. Nitrogen fixation is the process whereby elemental nitrogen is removed from the atmosphere by soil bacteria called rhizobia. These bacteria live in the nodules on roots of legume plants such as alfalfa, clover, peas, beans and vetch. Through the process, legumes can provide their own nitrogen supply; nitrogen converted to nitrates and is then part of the soil solution and available to the plants.

- **Nitrification** – Certain bacteria can transform nitrogen (in the form of ammonium) into nitrates. Nitrification is the biological oxidation of ammonia or ammonium to nitrite followed by the oxidation of the nitrite to nitrate. Nitrification is an important step in the nitrogen cycle in soil. Nitrogen is produced by the decomposition of proteins. The nitrates produced during this process are once again converted into proteins. Warm, moist, non-acid and well-aerated soil increases nitrification, while cold temperatures, below 50°F will inhibit nitrification.

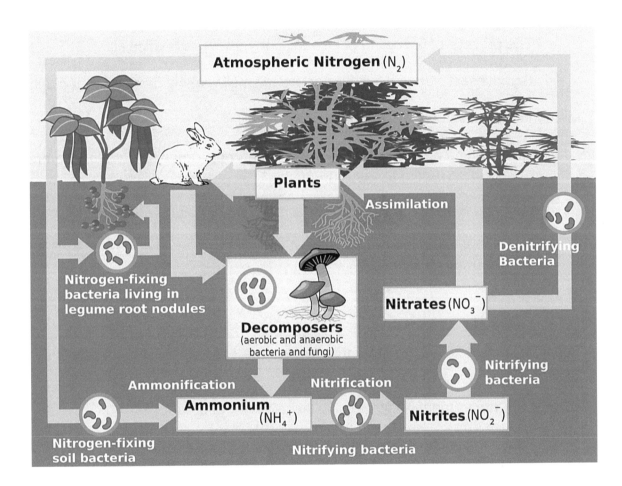

- **Denitrification**: Reverse process of nitrification

  - ✓ Nitrates are reduced to nitrites, then to nitrogen gas and ammonia.

  - ✓ Soil micro-organisms obtain oxygen from nitrates and nitrites then release nitrogen or nitrous oxide to the atmosphere.

  - ✓ Soils with high organic matter, waterlogged or poorly drained have a higher rate of denitrification; nitrogen in the soil is lost to the atmosphere, plant growth negatively impacted by loss of needed nutrients.

✓ Process has ecological importance as without denitrification, toxic forms of nitrogen (NO_3) would accumulate in the soil and water.

- Chemical breakdown

  o Organisms living in the soil can break down chemical refuse left in the soil.

    ✓ Microorganisms prevent a buildup of agricultural chemicals in the soil.

    ✓ The process of biological decomposition removes chemicals.

    ✓ Some insecticide use fails due to organisms breaking them down too quickly.

- Methane Production and Absorption

  o Methane can be produced during certain anaerobic organisms during the break down of organic matter in oxygen-free sites.

    ✓ Methane (swamp gas) is a major component of natural gas fuel.

    ✓ During their metabolic process, aerobic soil bacteria oxidize methane turning it into carbon dioxide (CO_2).

Soil Organisms Management

- Soil organisms and their habitat management are essential to a successful soil ecosystem.

  o **Inoculation** – Beneficially infecting soil with useful organisms

    ✓ Bacteria can be introduced to plants. Inoculation of first time legume crops with bacteria (rhizobia) has long been an important farming practice.

    ✓ Not always successful: Microbes added to soil sometimes do not survive due to competition with native flora.

    ✓ Products can be purchased that introduce soil organisms to soil, however, soil biologists recommend the nurturing of existing soil organism communities rather than introducing purchased external organisms.

- Ways to Encourage Beneficial Soil Organisms

  o Add organic matter (compost, mulch, manure, etc.) to the soil surface to be used as food for existing soil organisms.

- Water effectively. Soil organisms prefer a damp environment. Over-irrigation, however, will deprive them of oxygen (water-logged).

- Use pesticides carefully. Many fungicides, insecticides, and herbicides can kill or harm soil organisms.

- Good aeration means good oxygen supply, necessary for most organisms to thrive.

- Neutral pH is usually best, except for potatoes which are typically grown in acidic soils to control growth of a certain harmful actinomycete.

- Reduced tillage helps maintain organism population. Tillage reduces surface litter and directly kills many arthropods.

- Minimize fallowing. Fallowing, the practice of leaving crop land unseeded for one or more growing seasons, removes a soil organism's food source thereby eradicating them.

- Controlling Harmful Organisms

  - In severe cases of infestation soil sterilant chemicals are used.

  - Solarization is a non-chemical method used to sterilize the soil. Clear, plastic sheeting is placed over the soil in sunny weather for several weeks.

  > The above methods are effective in killing the harmful organisms, but kill the beneficial organisms along with the bad. Prevention and alternate methods are recommended when possible.

  - Crop rotation can sometimes suppress disease. If a harmful organism is specific to a certain crop, for instance, changing that crop will take away that organism's source of food, thereby eliminating it.

  - Bringing in large amounts of organic matter can sometimes correct a parasite problem as the new organisms that grow will compete with the parasites and may even fight them off altogether.

Animals in the Soil

- Many animals make their home in soil. While organisms affect cultivated soil more than animals, undisturbed soil can be heavily changed by animals.

  - Rodents mix the soil layers when they burrow. This action rejuvenates the soil.

- Prairie dog burrows reach depths of up to five feet in the ground. Subsoil is carried to the surface and mixed with the topsoil.

- Other burrowing animals include: gophers, moles, rabbits, snakes, badgers and woodchucks.

- Burrows may decrease erosion because surface water goes down into the holes and tunnels.

- These animals are typically considered pests in the agricultural community as they damage crops, roots and tunnel through fields.

Summary

Soil is home to a living ecosystem – the soil food web – includes organisms plus nutrients, plants and soil animals. Decomposition of living and dead organic matter results in necessary nutrients for plants and other soil organisms. Soil is an important part of the biological carbon cycle. Soil organisms, which can be categorized, vary greatly in size and complexity. They can be categorized by ecological function, trophic levels, primary producers or autotrophs, and heterotrophs which are the consumers in food chains. Soil organisms can also be grouped by their preferred environment – aerobic and anaerobic. A common classification of soil organisms is by taxonomy and size: macrofauna (ex. earthworms), mesofauna (ex. arthropods), nematodes (ex. non-segmented worms) and microfauna (ex. Protozoa). Microfauna are the smallest of soil organisms and are viewed under the microscope. The three main forms of microflora are bacteria, fungi and viruses. Also included are algae because of their chlorophyll-bearing organisms and actinomycetes which decompose resistant organic matter and form symbiotic nitrogen fixing relationships with many plant families. Nitrogen fixation, nutrient cycling, immobilization, nitrification and denitrification are all part of the functions of microorganisms. There are several ways to manage soil organisms – inoculation of useful organisms, encouraging beneficial organisms by addition of organic matter, watering effectively, careful use of pesticides, reducing tillage, crop rotation, controlling harmful organisms and minimizing fallowing. Animals in the soil can mix topsoil and subsoil but generally they are considered pests in the agricultural community as they damage crops and roots with tunneling.

Additional Resources

Plaster, E.J. 2013. Soil science and management. 6th Ed. Clifton Park, NY: Delmar, Cengage Learning.

National Resources Conservation Service
http://www.nrcs.usda.gov/wps/portal/nrcs/site/national/home/

Soil and Water Conservation Society
http://www.swcs.org/

Soil Biology
http://www.blm.gov/wo/st/en.html

Soil Science Society of America
https://www.soils.org/

USDA's Soil Biology Primer
http://soils.usda.gov/sqi/concepts/soil_biology/biology.html

Assessment

 Take the online assessment here: https://goo.gl/5TvCgx
Download and print the expanded written assessment by scanning this QR code or by going to this URL: https://www.tagmydoc.com/Ch05

Notes:

6 Organic Matter

Major Concept

Soil organic matter contains animal and plant remains at different stages of decay playing a critical role in plant growth and production.

Objectives

- Define what organic matter is and how it forms
- Name three benefits of organic matter
- List three benefits of humus
- Identify three parts of decomposition
- Define the five factors affecting organic matter
- Name three ways organic matter functions in the soil
- List four ways to maintain soil organic matter
- Define the carbon and nitrogen ratio
- Name two ways to use peat

Key Terms

- Carbon-nitrogen ratio
- Detritus
- Humification

- Humus
- Lignin
- Organic matter

- Muck
- Peat
- Soil aggregates

Chapter Resource

 Complementary *full color* illustrations, photos, charts and graphs are available by scanning this QR code or by following this URL: https://www.tagmydoc.com/SS06 These digital resources will enhance your understanding of the chapter concepts.

What is Organic Matter?

- **Organic matter** consists of plant and animal residues in various stages of decay. Adequate levels benefit soil in four ways:

    1. Improves physical condition and structure

    2. Increases water infiltration

    3. Decreases erosion losses

4. Supplies plant nutrients

- Can be grouped into three major types based on composition:

   1. Living microbial biomass, including microorganisms, and plant residue

   2. **Detritus** – active soil organic matter

   3. **Humus** – stable organic matter left in soil when plants or animals die

- The breakdown of the first two types of organic matter results in the release of nitrogen, phosphorous and potassium (which are nutrients for plants).

- The humus portion has less of a contribution to soil fertility as it is the final product of decomposition; important because it helps with the structure of soil, soil tilth, and cation exchange capacity; a more resistant residue from decay.

- **Humification** – Compounds formed from chemical reaction with soil nitrogen that is large, rich in nitrogen, highly complex and resistant to attack.

- Benefits of Humus:

   - Physical benefits: Assists with stability of aggregates, improves water filtration, soil aeration, reduces runoff, water holding capacity increased, reduces stickiness of clay soils making tilling easier, and reduced surface crusting.

   - Chemical benefits: Increases soil's CEC or its ability to hold onto and supply nutrients (calcium, magnesium, potassium), able to resist pH change or buffering capacity, and soil decomposition of minerals is accelerated making plant uptake of nutrients easier. **Note:** Cation Exchange Capacity (CEC) is the soil's capacity to hold exchangeable cations. CEC influences whether a soil can hold onto essential nutrients, provides a buffer against soil acidification, and is a measure of a soil's ability to hold positively charged ions.

   - Biological benefits: Provides food for soil organisms, soil microbial biodiversity activity is enhanced helping with disease and pest suppression, and pore space is enhanced helping infiltration to increase and runoff to be reduced.

   - Organic matter containing long chains of carbon atoms such as hydrogen, oxygen, nitrogen, and sulfur attach to the carbon chains to form organic compounds.

   - Plants provide carbohydrates in the form of starches, sugars and cellulose as food for soil microflora.

- o **Lignins**

  - ✓ Makes up most of soil humus

  - ✓ Large, highly complex molecules, 10-30% of plant tissue

  - ✓ Makes plants rigid and decay resistant

  - ✓ Contain no nitrogen

- Decomposition

  - o Decomposition and decay of organic matter occurs in stages:

    - ✓ Soil flora digests organic materials, releases carbon dioxide and water. Simpler compounds are produced, some of which become part of the soil humus.

    - ✓ Humus that is formed decays very slowly.

    - ✓ Fresh debris becomes soil organic matter by the process of decay. Depending on the chemical structure of the debris, decomposition can be rapid (sugars, starches, proteins), slow (cellulose, fats, waxes, and resins), or very slow (lignin).

    - ✓ Decay follows a series of intersecting steps:

      - ▪ Free amino acids and sugars, along with potassium and other water-soluble components dissolve quickly out of litter into nearby soil water.

      - ▪ Feeding on the organic matter and microbes, small mites and worms shred the material breaking through any protective coverings.

      - ▪ Shredded materials are split into even smaller units and become oxidized.

      - ▪ Carbon dioxide (CO_2) is produced and nutrients, like nitrogen (N) are liberated.

Additions and Losses

- The amount of organic matter in soil is the result of two processes:

  1. The addition of organic matter (roots, surface residue, crop residue, manure, etc.)

  2. The loss of organic matter through decomposition

- Factors affecting both additions and losses to organic matter are:

  ○ **Management**: Activities (irrigation, cover crops) that increase plant growth will increase root and crop residue, thereby increasing organic matter. Conversely, a field that is intensively tilled will lose organic matter.

  ○ **Soil Texture**: Fine-textured soils hold more organic matter than sandy soils. Clay particles form electrochemical bonds are able to hold organic compounds. Decomposition rates are faster in well-aerated sandy soils resulting in less organic matter.

  ○ **Climate**: High temperatures negatively affect organic matter by speeding up decomposition; high precipitation or irrigation provides more plant growth which means more roots and plant residues enter the soil, increasing the amount of organic matter.

  ○ **Landscape Position**: Areas that are poorly drained and low elevation have higher levels of organic matter due to less oxygen availability. Low areas are often where eroded organic matter from hill tops and slopes ends up.

  ○ **Vegetation**: In prairies, organic matter comes from deep grass roots; forest organic matter comes from the surface plant litter; farmland once prairie, will have higher amounts of organic matter at a deeper level as compared to lands that were previously forest.

Organic Matter Function in the Soil

- Organic matter functions in soil as nutrient and water storage, soil aggregation and erosion prevention; loosens clay soils and improves tilth.

- Nutrients are stored by organic matter through colloids and as part of their chemical makeup.

  ○ Humus and fresh organic matter absorb water like a sponge, holding approximately six times their weight.

  ○ Humus makes nutrients more available for plants.

- Organic matter decays, releasing organic acids which, in turn, dissolve soil minerals making it possible for plants to absorb nutrients.

- Chelation: Humus molecules form a ring around nutrient atoms such as iron and zinc, protecting these atoms from being locked in the soil and allowing them to become available for plants.

- Organic matter causes soil particles to cluster together forming soil aggregates.

- o **Soil aggregates** are groups of soil particles that bind to each other more strongly than to adjacent particles.

- o Spaces within and between soil aggregates are essential for storing air and water, microbes, nutrients and organic matter.

- o Soil microorganisms excrete substances that act as cementing agents and bind soil particles together.

- **Erosion Prevention**: Higher water infiltration means less water runoff that could remove soil. Erosion is slowed by soil high in organic matter because of water absorption and infiltration.

- Majority of nitrogen in soil is stored in organic matter.

- Sandy soils benefit greatly from organic matter and its ability to hold nutrients and water.

- Several different ways to maintain soil organic matter are listed in the table below:

Conservation Tillage	▪ Reduces influx of oxygen into the soil by leaving the crop residue to decay slowly on the surface (resulting in organic rich topsoil) ▪ Crusting and erosion reduced ▪ Improves moisture filtration
Crop Residue	▪ Leaving crop residues in the soil increases organic matter ▪ 1/3 of crop residue is typically harvested for use as animal feed, animal bedding, or fuel
Green Manure	▪ Crops are planted to be turned into the soil rather than to be harvested ▪ Reduces erosion and offers weed control
Cover Cropping	▪ Used to prevent erosion of soil in winter ▪ Crops such as winter rye or oats are planted in the fall after the main crop is harvested
Crop Rotation	▪ Rotating types of crops improves soil humus, maintains high level of organic matter ▪ Repeating same crop annually reduces soil organic matter ▪ Planting legume crops will increase organic matter by providing nitrogen to aid in decomposition of fresh organic materials
Adding Organic Matter	▪ Adding animal manure, organic waste, sewage sludge, or compost to the soil ▪ Improves soil aggregation and amount of plant-available nitrogen ▪ Composting is when organic material is stored in a pile on the ground under conditions that increase decay
Mulch	▪ Spreading straw, sawdust, or woodchips several inches deep on the ground ▪ As organic matter decays, humus content is enriched adding organic matter to soil ▪ Helps regulate soil temperature and limit water evaporation

Carbon and Nitrogen in Soil

- Plant growth requires carbon (energy) and nitrogen (for protein) in organic matter.

- The **C:N ratio** measures carbon to nitrogen.

  o Best ratio is 25:1- 25 parts of carbon to 1 part of nitrogen.

    ✓ Plant growth is best if soil is nitrogen rich, otherwise they do not thrive.

    ✓ Plant growth is slowed as organisms compete for nitrogen.

    ✓ Nitrogen is used to break down carbon sources; organic matter with high carbon content makes nitrogen unavailable to plants.

    ✓ When fresh organic matter is added or increased, the number of organisms rises which competes with crop plants for the available nitrogen causing plant growth to slow.

- Avoiding Nitrogen Losses

  o Planting crops after the decay of the previous crop residue is mostly complete.

  o Fertilizing the soil with enough nitrogen to provide the needs of the microorganisms that increased because of the fresh organic matter.

- Carbon-nitrogen ratios of some materials (lower ratio indicates richer nitrogen content):

o	Wood ashes	25:1
o	Alfalfa	12:1
o	Manures	15:1
o	Corn stalks	60:1
o	Sawdust	325:1
o	Garden waste	30:1
o	Food waste	20:1
o	Clover residue	23:1
o	Straw	75:1

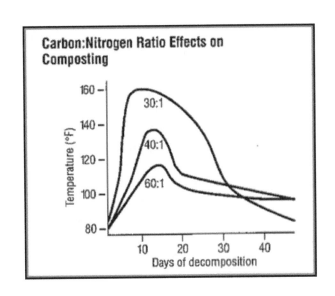

- Organic Soils (Histosols)

  o The organic matters previously discussed are those found in mineral soils. Organic soils contain more than 20 to 30% of organic matter.

    ✓ Found in swamps, bogs and marshes.

- ✓ The high amount of organic matter occurs when aquatic vegetation dies and sinks to the bottom.

- ✓ Because there is no air for decaying to occur, material continues to build up

- ✓ Breakdown is brought about by fungi and anaerobic bacteria.

- o **Peat** consists of plant remains partially decomposed in soil.

  - ✓ Can be dried and used as a fuel or heat source

  - ✓ Can be added to mineral soils to improve structure and increase acidity

  - ✓ Is not fertile but can store nutrients

- o **Muck** is organic material that is rotten, highly decomposed; often slimy and black in color.

  - ✓ Muck can be turned into a growing medium (potting soil) after the wetland is drained.

- o Crops can be grown directly on the organic soil (once drained); good for sod farm or turf grass, onions, celery, lettuce, carrots, mint and hay.

Summary

Organic matter consists of plant or animal tissue in varied stages of decomposition. In agriculture, a soil that is 3 to 6% organic matter is ideal. Based on composition, organic matter can be microorganisms, detritus, or humus. There are physical, chemical and biological benefits of humus in the interactions as part of decomposition. Decomposition occurs in several stages depending on the chemical structure of the matter. Organic matter functions in the soil as nutrient and water storage, soil aggregation and to prevent erosion. Several factors affecting additions and losses to organic matter are: management, soil texture, climate, landscape position and vegetation. There are several ways to maintain soil organic matter such as conservation tillage, crop residue and rotation, mulching, and cover cropping. Carbon and nitrogen are needed in organic matter for plant growth. This is expressed as the C:N ratio – the lower the ratio, the richer the nitrogen content. Some organic matter is found in swamps and marshes such as peat and muck. With drainage, these can be used for growing mediums.

Additional Resources

Plaster, E.J. 2013. Soil science and management. 6th ed. Clifton Park, NY: Delmar, Cengage Learning.

Troeh, F.R. and L.M. Thompson. 2005. Soils and soil fertility. 6th Ed. Ames, IA: Blackwell Publishing.

National Resources Conservation Service
http://www.nrcs.usda.gov/wps/portal/nrcs/site/national/home/

Soil and Water Conservation Society
http://www.swcs.org/

Soil Science Society of America
https://www.soils.org/

Assessment

Take the online assessment here: https://goo.gl/FToazs
Download and print the assessment by scanning this QR code or by going to this URL:https://www.tagmydoc.com/Ch06

Notes:

7 Soil Water

Major Concept

Understanding the importance of water in soil helps to improve water management for plant growth.

Objectives

- List four ways why soil water is important
- Name three factors in determining soil moisture
- Define the difference between temporary wilting point and permanent wilting point
- Identify the differences among gravitation water, capillary water and hygroscopic water
- Define four ways water can move through soil
- Discuss the role evapotranspiration has in soil and plants
- Identify the difference between cohesion and adhesion as a force on soil water
- Describe two ways to measure soil moisture

Key Terms

- Adhesion
- Capillarity
- Capillary rise
- Cohesion
- Gravitational potential
- Gravitational water
- Hygroscopic water
- Infiltration
- Matric potential
- Osmotic potential
- Percolation
- Permanent Wilting Point (PWP)
- Permeability
- Preferential flow
- Resistance block
- Runoff
- Saturated flow
- Temporary Wilting Point (TWP)
- Tensiometer
- Tension
- Transpiration
- Unsaturated flow

Chapter Resource

Complementary *full color* illustrations, photos, charts and graphs are available by scanning this QR code or by following this URL: https://www.tagmydoc.com/SS07 These digital resources will enhance your understanding of the chapter concepts.

Importance of Soil Water

- Makes up the major part of a growing plant – 45 to 95%.

- Photosynthesis uses water to manufacture carbohydrates.

- Necessary for the processes of transpiration and evapotranspiration and other chemical reactions.

- Responsible for turgor pressure

- Soil water is a nutrient.

- Aids in soil formation and weathering

- Helps to regulate soil temperature

Soil Moisture

- Factors determining the amount of moisture in soil include:

  o Amount of snow, rain or irrigation

  o Evaporation rate

  o Humidity levels

  o Water table – the depth of the natural level of the water below the surface of the soil

The Water Table

  o Amount and type of vegetation

  o Rate which soil permits water entry and the rate water moves within the soil

Soil Water Stress

- Water shortage

o Occurs as soil dries and becomes difficult for plants to absorb moisture.

   ✓ **Temporary Wilting Point (TWP)** - When plants lose water faster than it can be absorbed; plants can recover when conditions improve.

   ✓ **Permanent Wilting Point (PWP)** - When soil becomes too dry for the plant to access any water and cannot recover.

- Water Excess

   o Air shifts from soil pores causing deficiency of oxygen in the soil.

   o Roots lacking oxygen fail to absorb water and nutrients.

   o Fungal diseases attack damaged plant roots.

   o Carbon dioxide (CO_2) and toxic materials build up in the soil.

Chapter
Resource

Soil Water Classifications

- **Gravitational water**

   o Moves into, through or out of the soil under the influence of gravity.

   o Found in the macropores; moves rapidly out of well-drained soil (two to three days); can cause flooding in other areas.

   o Occupies air space in the pore spaces, can deprive oxygen to roots, causing plants to wilt and even die.

   o Water-soluble nutrients, chemicals and salts are "leached" out of the soil.

- Capillary water

   o A combination of cohesion, adhesion and surface tension forces.

   o Water is free to move from particle to particle in opposition to external forces (i.e.: gravity).

   o Most important component of soil moisture available to plants; most, but not all, of capillary water is available for plant growth.

- **Hygroscopic water**

  - Water absorbed from the atmosphere forming a very thin film around soil particles which cannot be taken up by the plant roots.

Water Movement and Retention in the Soil

- Water Retention

  - **Moisture-holding capacity** is a term describing a soil's ability to retain water.

  - **Infiltration** is the movement of water into soil.

  - Soil contains pores that vary in size and determine water retention-large pores holding water loosely and small pores holding water tightly; conduit allowing water to infiltrate and percolate; storage compartment for water.

  - **Tension** is a measure of how much suction the soil pore exerts on water.

  - Average soil is made up of about 25% water.

  - The optimum condition for plant growth is soil that has a combination of micropores and mesopores for water storage and macropores for gas exchange with the atmosphere.

- Water Movement

  - **Capillarity** – the primary force that enables the soil to retain water, as well as to regulate its movement. Capillarity is the tendency of a liquid in a capillary tube or absorbent material to rise or fall because of surface tension.

  - **Saturated Flow** (gravitational) – Water flows downward by gravity; occurs mainly in large soil pores.

  - **Unsaturated Flow (capillary)** – Water flows primarily by capillary action (multi-directional) from moist to dry soil; or from areas of high potential to areas of low potential called **capillary rise.**

  - **Percolation** is the downward movement of water within the soil.

  - **Permeability** indicates the quality of soil allowing both kinds of water movement.

  - **Preferential flow** is flow of free water through large pores, bypassing the general soil matrix.

✓ Greatly increases infiltration and percolation, reducing runoff and allowing deeper penetration of water.

✓ Deeper penetration of pollutants such as pesticides because the water bypasses the filtering action of the soil matrix.

Loss of Water in Soil

- Major losses of soil water are through transpiration by plants and evaporation from soil surface through the process of evapotranspiration (ET).

  o ET can be affected by weather, crop type, crop growth stage, crop variety, crop population, surface cover, tillage and water availability.

  o **Transpiration** – Evaporative process where water turns to vapor and is released from plants through the stomata (tiny pores) in their leaves.

  o Harvested crops – Many crops contain high levels of moisture which is carried away with the crop when harvested.

- **Runoff** – Excess water that flows over the ground.

Ways of Increasing Soil Water Availability for Crops

- Growing more drought-resistant crop varieties and cultivars.

- Installing more efficient irrigation systems.

- Lessening nonproductive evaporation through mulching or decreasing the areas of exposed water surface.

- Reusing return flows.

- Using alternative freeze protection methods.

- Minimizing nonproductive depletion of water flow such as through canal and reservoir lining.

Forces on Soil Water

- Several forces acting on soil water are –

  o **Adhesion** – The force of attraction between unlike molecules (water to soil particles).

- ✓ Water molecules are strongly attracted to soil minerals and organic materials due to adhesion.

- ✓ Water held by adhesion is not available to the plant.

- o **Cohesion** – The force of attraction between like molecules (water molecules to other water molecules).

  - ✓ Water molecules are strongly attracted to each other due to cohesion.

  - ✓ Water held by cohesion is available to the plant.

- o Soil-water potential

  - ✓ How much work a plant will have to do to extract water from the soil.

  - ✓ The lower the soil-water potential, the more tightly water is attracted to soil particles and the less freely it can move.

  - ✓ Higher soil-water potential means water more available to plant.

  - ✓ Can consist of several separate actions:

    - ▪ **Matric potential** – Results from the attraction of water molecules to soil particles; determines movement of soil water and water availability to plants.

    - ▪ **Gravitational potential** – When soil water is above water table level and carries potential energy by gravity.

    - ▪ **Osmotic potential** – Refers to the attraction of salts and dissolved organic compounds (solutes) to water.

Measuring Soil Moisture

- • Several ways to measure water in a soil:

  - o Gravimetric measurements

    - ✓ Taking a soil sample, weighing it, drying in an oven (220°F for 24 hours) and then re-weighing the sample to determine what was lost.

  - o Feel method – Soil is evaluated by feeling the soil; only an estimate; developed over time with extensive use

- Portable soil moisture probe – Several types available with electronic meters which can use resistance or capacitance technology (ability to story electrical charge).

- **Tensiometer** or potentiometer is a sealed, airtight, water-filled tube with a porous tip on one end and a vacuum gauge on the other end which measures soil water suction expressed as tension.

- **Resistance block** – A meter is used to read the electrical resistance of moisture blocks installed in the ground; the blocks incorporate two electrodes imbedded in a gypsum material and covered with a porous material; porous material allows water to move in equilibrium with the soil moisture indicating changes in amount of water in soil.

Summary

Soil water is required for the function and maintenance of growing plants. Several factors aid in soil moisture such as the amount of snow and rain, evaporation rate, humidity levels, the amount and type of vegetation and the rate soil allows movement of water. Soil stress occurs with a shortage or excess of water. Water can move through the soil by gravitational flow, capillary or hygroscopic movement. Water is held in the soil by tension and pore size. It can move through the soil by percolation, preferential flow, saturated or unsaturated or capillary flow or by the permeability of the soil. Major loses of soil water are through evapotranspiration which can be affected by weather, crop type, crop growth stage, crop variety, crop population, surface cover, tillage and water availability. Several ways are possible to increase soil water. Other forces on soil water are adhesion and cohesion which determine the attraction of water to soil making water more or less available to plants. Several ways to measure water in soil are through gravimetric, feel method, tensiometer, or resistance blocks.

Additional Resources

Brady, N.C. and R. Weil. 2007. Nature and properties of soil. 14th ed. Englewood Cliffs, NJ: Prentice Hall.

Parker, R. 2010. Plant and Soil Science. Clifton Park, NY: Delmar Publishing.

Plaster, E.J. 2013. Soil science and management. 6th ed. Clifton Park, NY: Delmar, Cengage Learning.

National Resources Conservation Service
http://www.nrcs.usda.gov/wps/portal/nrcs/main/national/soils/health/

Soil and Water Conservation Society
http://www.swcs.org/

Soil Science Society of America
https://www.soils.org/

Assessment

 Take the online assessment here: https://goo.gl/mPJyac
Download and print the expanded written assessment by scanning this QR code or by going to this URL: https://www.tagmydoc.com/Ch07

Notes:

8 Water Conservation

Major Concept

Water quality and availability is critical to plant health and growth.

Objectives

- Define the hydrologic cycle or water cycle
- Name three forms of precipitation
- Explain the difference between an unconfined and confined aquifer
- List two ways of improving water-use efficiency
- Define the three categories of water saving irrigation practices
- Name two ways to improve water infiltration
- Explain two methods to capture water runoff
- Define consumptive use of water
- Name two ways to improve water-use efficiency
- List three ways to avoid chemical water pollution
- Explain the difference between point and nonpoint source pollution

Key Terms

- Antitranspirants
- Aquifer
- Consumptive use
- Furrow-diking
- Groundwater
- Hydrologic cycle
- Hydrophilic gel polymers
- Nonpoint source pollution
- Point source pollution
- Precipitation
- Runoff
- Soil pitting
- Subsoiling
- Surface water
- Water-use efficiency

Chapter Resource

Complementary *full color* illustrations, photos, charts and graphs are available by scanning this QR code or by following this URL: https://www.tagmydoc.com/SS08 These digital resources will enhance your understanding of the chapter concepts.

Hydrologic Cycle

- The **hydrologic cycle**, or water cycle, refers to the movement of water on, above and within the earth.

- Water moves by means of different processes: evaporation, condensation, precipitation, infiltration, runoff and subsurface flow; and goes through different physical phases: liquid, solid (ice), and gas (vapor).

  ○ As the sun heats the ocean's water, some of it evaporates into the air as vapor. The vapor rises into the air where cooler temperatures cause it to condense into clouds.

  ○ Water released from clouds in the form of rain, freezing rain, sleet, snow or hail is **precipitation.**

  ○ When precipitation lands on the soil it proceeds through the hydrologic cycle by several ways:

    ✓ **Runoff** – Rainfall or snowmelt that runs over the top of the ground and cannot be absorbed into soil quickly.

    ✓ Infiltration which is affected by soil characteristics such as land cover, evapotranspiration, water table, slope of land or amount of precipitation.

    ✓ Water stored in the soil can evaporate from the surface back into the atmosphere or go further in to the ground into an aquifer.

    ✓ Evaporation, which is the primary mechanism supporting the surface to atmosphere portion of the water cycle. On a global scale, the amount of water evaporating is about the same as the amount of water delivered to the earth as precipitation.

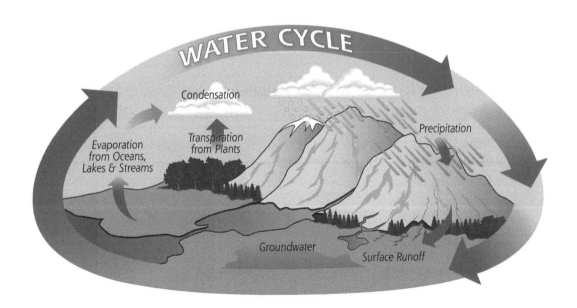

Water Resources

- Stored water sources

  - Snow, ice and glaciers; about 69% of the world's fresh **surface water** is in glaciers and ice caps

  - Deep groundwater storage

- Fresh surface water

  - Annual rainfall varies widely from area to area therefore many states rely on irrigation to grow crops.

  - Besides rainfall, balance of precipitation and evapotranspiration is an important factor in determining if irrigation is needed.

  - Occupies streams, lakes, rivers, wetlands, reservoirs and ponds and covers approximately 60 million acres of U.S. farm land.

  - Distributed unequally; most surface water is in the Great Lakes and a few other states, especially Alaska, Texas, Minnesota, Florida and North Carolina.

  - In western states, surface water for irrigation and other uses depends on rivers fed by snowmelt in mountains.

- Groundwater

  - Two major societal concerns are: lack of potable drinking water and need for water for irrigation to support agriculture. Groundwater is the major provider of these. Groundwater is water than has seeped into the ground through rocks, cracks and soil.

  - Ninety-nine percent of groundwater is stored in underground formations called **aquifers**.

    - ✓ Aquifers are underground layers of rock and sediment saturated with water; water exists in most places under the earth's surface; two types of aquifers are:

      1. Confined aquifer: Water supply is sandwiched between two impermeable layers.

      2. Unconfined aquifer: Contains unpressurized groundwater; has an impermeable layer below it but not above it; is the most common type.

Chapter Resource

- ✓ Water from aquifers can be brought to the surface naturally through springs or by drilling a well and pumping the water out.

- ✓ Some aquifers have parts that can recharge and are replenished when precipitation is above-average levels, but the long term trend is moving towards depletion.

- ○ Groundwater renews very slowly, averaging about 3 inches per year.

- ○ According to the USDA, about 25% of the U.S. groundwater supplies are being "mined" and water is being withdrawn more rapidly than it is renewed. This is leading to a possible water shortage crisis and is creating higher water expenses for farmers and water users which in turn lead to higher food prices.

- Reasons for conservation of water resources

  - ○ Approximately 70% of the world's water is being used for irrigation; 15 to 35% of these withdrawals are unsustainable.

  - ○ The USDA forecasts that within thirty years, 6.6 million acres of land currently being irrigated using groundwater mining will no longer be able to be used for agriculture because of dwindling water availability.

  - ○ There are many benefits to agricultural conservation efforts: Preservation of water resources, increased crop yields and fewer problems from runoff.

- Water-use efficiency

  - ○ Of the water that lands on a field, most is lost to runoff, percolation or evapotranspiration.

  - ○ **Water-use efficiency** can be measured by the amount of water needed to produce a unit of dry plant matter.

  - ○ Ways of improving water-use efficiency:

    - ✓ Capturing more of the water from precipitation in the root zone of crop plants by improving the infiltration rate and reducing percolation.

    - ✓ Reducing consumptive use - the sum of the water lost by evapotranspiration and the amount contained in plant tissues.

    - ✓ Improving irrigation systems.

Water Saving Practices

- Water saving irrigation practices fall into three categories:

  1. Field practices – keep more water in the soil, reducing irrigation needs. Examples are: chiseling compacted soils, furrow diking to prevent runoff, leveling land for even distribution of water.

  2. Management strategies – involve practicing awareness of soil and water conditions by measuring rainfall and soil moisture and adjusting irrigation schedules accordingly.

  3. System modifications – means purchasing or modifying equipment to cut down water usage. Example: adding drop tubes to a center pivot system or constructing a tailwater recovery system.

- Water reusing/recycling

  o Water reuse for irrigation is already in widespread use in rural areas and is also applicable in areas where agricultural sites are near urban areas and can easily be integrated with urban reuse applications (USEPA, 1992).

  o Water Reusing – Reusing wastewater (treated) or reclaimed water for another purpose (such as irrigation).

  o Water Recycling – Re-using water for the same purpose it was originally used for.

**Chapter
Resource**

- Improving infiltration/lowering percolation

  o To capture more water landing on a field a grower can improve infiltration and/or lower deep percolation.

  o Protection of soil surface porosity from rainfall impact

    ✓ Protective soil cover: mulch, crop residue, cover crop, avoid tillage

    ✓ Will reduce soil particle detachment, less clogging of surface pores

  o Improvement of soil structure through biological processes

    ✓ Add organic matter to the soil to increase biological activity; resulting in soil aggregates forming and stabilizing; higher resistance to disintegration/erosion

    ✓ Maintaining organic matter means maintaining a healthy, "water-retentive" topsoil.

- Using physical/structural barriers to decrease water run-off; utilizes physical or vegetative structures across the slope, and gives more time for infiltration to occur by capturing or slowing water runoff

- Methods for capturing water runoff:

  - Terrace – Series of low ridges and shallow channels running across a slope, gathering water and allowing it to seep in (rather than run-off).

  - **Furrow-diking** – Special equipment creates basins to hold water by making furrows with dikes (small ridges).

  - **Soil pitting** – Creating tiny pits to capture water.

  - Contour tillage – Tilling across the fields slope rather than up and down; process creates ridges that infiltrate water into the soil, decreases water runoff and soil erosion.

  - Strip-cropping – Alternating crops across the slope; row crops alternated with a close-growing crop or a crop that covers the soil decreasing water runoff.

- Methods for improving water intake:

  - **Subsoiling** – Deep chiseling; breaking up compacted soil layers found under the topsoil to allow roots deeper access.

  - Conservation tillage – Leaving crop residue on the soil surface as mulch; also called no-till.

  - **Hydrophilic gel polymers** increase water-holding capacity of soil; absorb and hold water many times their weight, not releasing it until soil has dried.

  - Capturing snowfall – A method used in northern areas to keep snow from blowing away.

- Buffer strips – Also called a snow fence, consists of leaving strips of a tall crop standing at right angles against the wind to stop snow from blowing away.

- Stubble mulching – Leaving crop stubble over the winter season to hold snow to the ground.

Chapter
Resource

- Cloud Seeding

- Cloud seeding is a weather modification method whereby substances are sent up into the air in an attempt to alter the microphysical processes within the clouds. The method, which is very expensive and has debatable success, seeks to control the amount and type of precipitation in a given area.

Consumptive Use

- **Consumptive use** is the total water used to produce a crop – including evaporation, transpiration and water that become part of the plant.

  - Warm air temperature, dry air (low humidity), and wind, increase transpiration from leaves and evaporation from the soil.

  - Plant efficiency for using water is related to a plant's health, root system, species, variety and nutritional status.

- Reducing soil water evaporation

  - Overall water usage can be reduced by reducing evaporation in the soil.

  - Higher temperatures speed up the evaporation process; keeping the soil cool, evaporation can be decreased.

  - Covering the soil surface with either vegetation or mulch, shading the soil, and reducing wind velocity at the soil surface help retain soil moisture

  - Reducing the number of tillage operations helps control evaporative losses.

  - Controlling weeds helps decrease water loss in the soil.

- Reducing transpiration

  - The amount of water lost through transpiration varies greatly depending on location and season; temperature, humidity level, and wind are all factors that determine rate of transpiration.

- Methods to reduce transpiration:

  - ✓ Planting windbreaks of taller plants or trees.

  - ✓ Eliminating weeds will lower moisture loss, because weeds also transpire.

  - ✓ Coating leaves with **antitranspirants,** a chemical material that reduces water loss through stomata and leaf surfaces by reducing the size and number of stomata. But with a downside: Photosynthesis is inhibited, negatively impacting plant growth.

- Improving water plant-use efficiency

  - The efficiency of plant water use can be measured by the transpiration ratio: The amount of water transpired divided by the amount of dry matter produced.

  - Great variation exists between plants in how much water they need; for example, alfalfa needs three times as much water to produce a pound of material as sorghum.

  - Good soil fertility and adequate levels of nitrogen and phosphorus improve water use by plants.

  - Use of plants adapted for growing under dry conditions (bred to be drought resistant) can improve plant efficiency; example is xeriscaping.

Water Quality

- In agricultural settings, preventative actions are taken when using chemicals, to prevent polluting water sources (streams, reservoirs, etc.).

  - Several ways to avoid water pollution by land users:

    - ✓ Reduce contaminated runoff and erosion containing contaminated soil.

    - ✓ Reduce fertilizer losses in percolating water.

    - ✓ Reduce use of pesticides by crop rotation and other strategies.

    - ✓ Apply and store manure properly.

    - ✓ Help reserve wetlands that filter pollutants from runoff.

  - What is nonpoint and point source pollution?

- ✓ **Nonpoint source pollution** usually comes from land runoff, precipitation, drainage, and seepage. Nonpoint source pollution can come from: Excess fertilizers, herbicides and insecticides from agricultural lands; salt from irrigation practices; and bacteria and nutrients from livestock waste. Agricultural sources of water pollution are typically considered to be a nonpoint source because they do not meet the legal requirements above.

- ✓ **Point source pollution**, as defined by the Clean Water Act, is any discernible, confined and discrete conveyance, including but not limited to any pipe, ditch, channel, tunnel, conduit, well, discrete fissure, container, rolling stock, concentrated animal feeding operation, or vessel or other floating craft, from which pollutants are or may be discharged.

Summary

The hydrologic cycle, or water cycle, refers to the movement of water on, above, and within the earth through the processes of evaporation, condensation, precipitation, infiltration, runoff and subsurface flow. Precipitation goes through the water cycle by runoff, infiltration and evaporation. Evaporation is the primary mechanism supporting the surface to atmosphere portion of the water cycle. There are many water resources such as lakes, reservoirs, ice and snow, aquifers and groundwater. Conservation of water is critical for irrigation for agriculture and human consumption. Ways to improve water use efficiently include capturing more water from precipitation, reducing consumptive use and improving irrigation systems. Three categories of water saving irrigation practices include field practices, management strategies and system modifications. Water can also be reused and recycled, and infiltration improved. There are several methods for improving water intake. Consumptive use is the total water used to produce a crop. Reducing soil water evaporation and transpiration varies greatly depending on plant and location. Good soil fertility and adequate levels of nitrogen and phosphorus improve water use by plants. Agriculturists continually work to prevent polluting water sources.

Additional Resources

Parker, R. 2010. Plant and soil science. Clifton Park, NY: Delmar Publishing

Plaster, E.J. 2013. Soil science and management. 6th ed. Clifton Park, NY: Delmar, Cengage Learning

Soil and Water Conservation Society
http://www.swcs.org/

Soil Science Society of America
https://www.soils.org/

National Resources Conservation Service
http://www.nrcs.usda.gov/wps/portal/nrcs/site/national/home/

Assessment

 Take the online assessment here: https://goo.gl/zXfGcw
Download and print the expanded written assessment by scanning this QR code or by going to this URL: https://www.tagmydoc.com/Ch08

Notes:

9 Irrigation and Drainage

Major Concept

Different types of irrigation systems fit different needs when providing water to crops and water holding capacity depends on soil type.

Objectives

- Name four types of irrigation systems
- List advantages and disadvantage of each type
- List three factors that influence the requirement for water
- Identify the concept of water holding (or field) capacity of different soils
- Define acre inch, acre foot, water penetration and water holding capacity
- List four factors that determine water penetration and water holding capacity of soil
- List three advantages of Scientific Irrigation Scheduling (SIS)

Key Terms

- Acre-foot
- Acre-inch
- Drainage
- Emitters
- Furrow method

- Irrigation
- Precipitation
- Rain-fed farming
- Scientific Irrigation Scheduling (SIS)

- Water Holding Capacity
- Water penetration

Chapter Resource

Complementary *full color* illustrations, photos, charts and graphs are available by scanning this QR code or by following this URL: https://www.tagmydoc.com/SS09 These digital resources will enhance your understanding of the chapter concepts.

History of Irrigation

- **Irrigation** is the artificial application of water to soil to supplement water available from rainfall and snow to help with crop production.

- All plants require water to live and grow. In many areas, rainfall is not sufficient to produce a crop. Irrigation has been necessary to supplement rainfall for over 7,000 years.

- Historical findings indicate crops were irrigated along the Euphrates, Ganges, Nile and Tigris rivers as early as 1800 B.C.

- Even though irrigation has been practiced for so many years, modern methods were started as little as 200 years ago.

- One factor in deciding on irrigation needs is precipitation forecast and history. The National Weather Service and the World Meteorological Organization both issue reports that monitor and predict expected rainfall.

- **Rain-fed farming** is the natural application of water to the soil through direct rainfall. This occurs in areas where there is enough precipitation to grow crops without irrigation. It is also common in poor, developing countries, where irrigation is not available.

Efficiency

- A key to efficient water use is to apply only enough water to meet full evapotranspiration of the crop.

- Water requirements of any given crop will vary depending on the following:

  - Weather: Air temperature, humidity, solar radiation, and wind have a big impact on increasing or decreasing soil evaporation and crop transpiration.

  - Crop Type: Different crops use different amounts of water over the course of the growing season.

  - Crop Growth Stage: Evapotranspiration is related to leaf surface area, therefore, a larger plant will transpire more and require more water. Conversely, as crops mature, their evapotranspiration decreases.

  - Crop Population: Having more plants per acre can help lower evaporation losses due to plants shading one another.

  - Surface Cover and Tillage: Evaporation is lowered by mulched soil surfaces. Crop residues left on fields can reduce soil evaporation by one to three inches.

  - Climate: In humid regions, the chance of rainfall occurring shortly after irrigation is high. Arid and semi-arid regions have low probabilities of precipitation and require more irrigation.

Chapter
Resource

Irrigation Systems

- Selection of the right watering system can save labor and water, and assure increased crop yields. Four basic irrigation methods are surface, sub-surface, drip and aerial (overhead or sprinkler).

    1. Surface irrigation methods include: Flooding, bed or border method, basin method, furrow method.

        ✓ Flooding: Opening a water channel; water released using gates, valves or siphons; water flows in all directions and floods field.

            ▪ Land must be leveled and graded; uniform slope of 0.1 to 0.4 feet per 100 feet.

            ▪ Typically, there is a great loss of water by runoff and deep percolation using this method.

        ✓ Bed or border method: Field is leveled; divided into small beds; small channels are dug between rows of beds.

        ✓ Basin method: Basin may be square or circular shape; field divided into small, level unit areas; ridges built forming basins.

        ✓ **Furrow method**: Water flows in furrows along contours or straight furrows; used in row crops. This method is efficient in water utilization.

    2. Subsurface irrigation: Natural or artificial.

        ✓ Natural subsurface irrigation occurs when water is present below the root zone; ditches allow water to move laterally.

        ✓ Artificial subsurface irrigation pipes are laid out underground below the root zone and water is raised by capillary movement.

    3. Drip irrigation: This system involves slow application of water into the plant's root zone using a: head, main line and subline, lateral lines and drip nozzles.

        ✓ Head: Has a pump causing pressure to lift water and distribute to nozzles.

        ✓ Mains and submains: Pipes to move water.

        ✓ Laterals or drip lines: Small diameter flexible lines taking off from mains/submains.

✓ **Emitters**: Device with pin-hole size openings located at intervals along lateral plastic tubes laid on soil surface.

✓ Drip nozzles: Emit water flow at slow rate.

4. Sprinkler/overhead irrigation: Applies water to soil in form of spray. System typically uses: Power generator, pump, pipeline and sprinkler.

✓ Main pipes usually made of steel or iron; pipes above ground or underground.

✓ Laterals are lightweight aluminum pipes that are typically portable.

✓ Sprinkler nozzles have a larger opening than drip systems. They are found on hand lines, wheel lines and center pivots.

✓ Three types of sprinklers: rotating, stationary spray-type nozzles and perforated pipe.

Ditch Maintenance

- Irrigation ditches require regular maintenance to improve water delivery.

  o In some states, regular spring burning is used to control weeds and grasses in ditches.

  o In some areas, a ditch company will collect fees from all irrigation water rights holders on that ditch. They then hire "ditch riders" to maintain the ditches and operate the main gates.

Irrigation System Considerations

- Irrigation systems vary in sophistication and cost to install and maintain; each system has its advantages and disadvantages.

  o There are many irrigation methods to choose from. These factors should be considered before deciding on a system:

    ✓ Proximity of the field or pasture to a water source

    ✓ Adequate distribution system to the field (pumps, canals or pipes)

    ✓ Amount of water required by selected crop

    ✓ Quality and cost of available water

    ✓ Topography of the land

✓ Soil type

✓ Annual precipitation

✓ Fertilization methods

✓ Methods for recycling or handling excess irrigation water

Scientific Irrigation Scheduling (SIS)

- **Scientific Irrigation Scheduling (SIS)** refers to a method of irrigating that measures the actual soil moisture and crop evapotranspiration and delivers water to the crops based on those scientific measurements.

  - SIS saves energy, water and fertilizer costs (less loss of fertilizer through leaching).

  - System monitors weather and soil moisture data with monitoring equipment.

  - SIS is most beneficial to agricultural irrigation systems with a pumping capacity beyond that required to meet normal crop needs.

Deciding When to Irrigate

- Determining soil moisture helps to make decisions regarding when to irrigate. Several methods were discussed in a previous chapter. These methods are gravimetric, the feel method, portable soil moisture probes, tensiometers or resistance blocks.

- Other methods to determine irrigation needs are evaporation pans, computer programs using metrological data to calculate water use along with forecasts and measuring water through water budgeting methods.

Water Measurements, Cost and Soil Capacity

- Water is measured for agricultural uses in acre feet.

  - An **acre-foot** of water is equal to approximately 326,000 gallons, or enough water to cover an acre of land one foot deep.

  - Individual crops require a varying amount of water to reach marketable size, stage or maturity, typically 16 to 36 inches of useable (available) water.

  - Rainfall is measured in inches of water precipitated.

- ✓ One inch of water in the form of rainfall over one acre, would be one "**acre-inch** of water."

- Cost of irrigation water varies widely throughout the U.S and the world.

  - In irrigation districts, the landowner is charged a given amount for each acre foot of water. For example:

    - ✓ Grower uses 1.75 acre feet of water. Cost is $50.00 per acre foot.

    - ✓ Total cost paid by the landowner is $87.50.

- In irrigated areas, growers supplement the natural **precipitation** (rain or snow) with irrigation water. For example:

  - If a crop requires 32 inches of water to reach maturity and rain supplied 12 inches, how much water would the grower have to add by irrigation?

  - 32 inches minus 12 inches = 20 inches of water needs to be added.

  - This would be the case for 100% efficiency of water use. (Seldom is this the case, the best efficiency rate is 85-90% and common is 65-75%)

- **Water holding capacity** is the total amount of water soil can hold at field capacity. Sandy soils tend to have low water storage capacity.

- Plant available water is the portion of the water holding capacity that can be absorbed by the plant (usually about 50%).

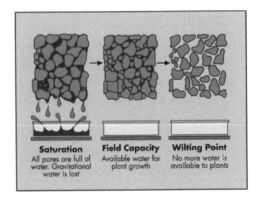

Saturation
All pores are full of water. Gravitational water is lost

Field Capacity
Available water for plant growth

Wilting Point
No more water is available to plants

  - Typical water holding capacities (water per foot of soil) varies according to the texture of the soil:

    - ✓ Finer texture soils have a greater water holding capacity.

    - ✓ Sandy soils have a lower water holding capacity but because of larger pores have better drainage and air movement.

    - ✓ Soils with a compacted surface have both lower water holding capacity and infiltration rate, leading to higher runoff and erosion.

    - ✓ Soils with high or added organic matter content tend to have a higher water holding capacity.

Textural class	Water holding capacity, inches/foot of soil
Coarse sand	0.25 - 0.75
Fine sand	0.75 - 1.00
Loamy sand	1.10 - 1.20
Sandy loam	1.25 - 1.40
Fine sandy loam	1.50 - 2.00
Silt loam	2.00 - 2.50
Silty clay loam	1.80 - 2.00
Silty clay	1.50- 1.70
Clay	1.20 - 1.50

- ○ Range of water-holding:

  - ✓ The depth to which irrigation water or rain penetrates the soil before the rate of downward movement becomes negligible is called **water penetration**.

  - ✓ This will vary with the type of soil. Typical ranges of penetration for each type of soil are:

    - ▪ 10 to 12 inches penetration in sand

    - ▪ 6 to 10 inches penetration in silt

    - ▪ 4 to 6 inches penetration in clay

- Factors affecting water penetration include:

  Chapter
  Resource

  - ○ Soil texture

  - ○ Organic matter content of the soil

  - ○ Presence of impermeable layers

  - ○ Amount of soil compaction

  - ○ Amount of surface crusting (1.25 to 2.0 inches per foot of clay soils)

Drainage

- Irrigation is often studied together with **drainage**, which is the natural or artificial removal of surface and sub-surface water from a given area. Ideally, excess water will drain from the soil so that roots will not be deprived of needed oxygen.

  - ○ Poor drainage

    - ✓ Waterlogged or "wet" soils can be caused by compacted clay, flooding or excess runoff from another area, or a high-water table.

    - ✓ Poorly drained fields can cause:

      - ▪ Damaged root tips, poor nutrient absorption and a buildup of toxic materials in the soil.

      - ▪ Delay to planting can occur, due to soil taking longer to dry; wet soil also stays cold later in season, possibly delaying planting and seed emergence.

o Artificial drainage – Surface and sub-surface

✓ Surface drainage entails digging a ditch for excess water to drain into.

✓ Subsurface drainage involves burying pipes for excess water to seep into. Water is discharged to an outlet.

Summary

Irrigation is the artificial application of water to soil to supplement water available from rainfall and snow to help with crop production. Even though irrigation practices have been around since 1800 BC, modern methods were started as little as 200 years ago. Water requirements of any given crop vary depending on weather, crop type, crop growth stage, crop population, surface cover and tillage and climate. Selecting the right watering system can save labor and water and assure increased crop yields. Surface methods of irrigation include flooding, bed or border, basin and furrow methods. Subsurface irrigation can be natural or artificial. Drip irrigation involves a slow application of water to the plant. Sprinkler/overhead irrigation uses pipes, nozzles and can be hand lines, wheel lines or center pivots. Watering using irrigation ditches requires that ditches be maintained. There are many irrigation systems which vary in cost, sophistication and maintenance. Each system has advantages and disadvantages and many factors should be considered to determine which system to use. One relatively new system – the scientific irrigation scheduling (SIS) – is a method of irrigating that measures the actual soil moisture and crop evapotranspiration and delivers water to the crops based on those scientific measurements. Water is measured for agricultural uses by acre feet and the cost to the landowner is determined using this measure. The water-holding capacity of a soil is an important consideration along with the natural or artificial drainage of water.

Additional Resources

Parker, R. 2010. Plant and soil science: Fundamentals and applications. Clifton Park, NY: Delmar Cengage Learning. pgs. 207-210.

Plant & Soil Science eLibrary: Soils - Part 2: Physical properties of soil and soil water
http://tinyurl.com/plant-library

Soil Moisture Measurement Technology
http://cecentralsierra.ucanr.edu/files/96233.pdf

Soil Irrigation
http://www.fao.org/docrep/r4082e/r4082e06.htm

Soil Drainage
http://www.fao.org/docrep/r4082e/r4082e07.htm#TopOfPage

Assessment

 Take the online assessment here: https://goo.gl/F1oqmz
Download and print the expanded written assessment by scanning this QR code or by going to this URL: https://www.tagmydoc.com/Ch09

Notes:

10 Soil Fertility

Major Concept

Good soil fertility can be achieved by understanding what promotes and increases soil quality for optimal plant productivity.

Objectives

- List six indicators of good soil quality
- Identify five aspects of good soil fertility
- Name three factors affecting soil fertility
- Name the non-mineral, primary and secondary plant nutrients
- Identify the difference between cations and anions
- Define the difference between acidic and alkaline
- Explain cation exchange capacity and how it determines soil use
- List the three types of soil colloids and define their role in plant nutrition
- Name four ways soil fertility is affected

Key Terms

- Adsorption
- Anion
- Base saturation
- Cation

- Cation exchange capacity (CEC)
- Exchangeable bases
- Micelle

- pH
- Soil colloids

Chapter Resource

Complementary *full color* illustrations, photos, charts and graphs are available by scanning this QR code or by following this URL: https://www.tagmydoc.com/SS10 These digital resources will enhance your understanding of the chapter concepts.

Soil Fertility

- Ability of soil to supply nutrients for plant growth. The following aspects apply:

  o Nutrient rich for basic nutrition

  o Sufficient minerals

  o Organic matter to improve soil structure and for moisture retention

- o Good pH balance of 6.0 to 7.0 range

- o Good soil structure for drainage

- o Microorganisms to support plant growth

- o Adequate amounts of topsoil

- Factors affecting soil fertility:

  - o Cation Exchange Capacity

  - o Nutrients stored

  - o Uptake of nutrients by roots

  - o Soil features such as oxygen supply, water supply and water temperature

  - o Soil temperature

  - o Soil pathogens

  - o The following table indicates factors affecting soil fertility:

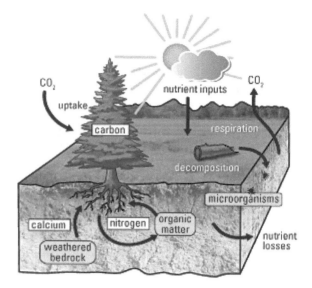

Raises Fertility	Lowers Fertility
High clay content	High sand content
High humus content	Loss of organic matter
Good structure	Compaction
Warm soil	Hot or cold soil
Deep soil	Shallow soil
Moist soil	Wet or dry soil
Good drainage	Excess irrigation / drainage
Fertilization	Erosion
Desirable microbes	Root damaging pests
Close to neutral pH	pH to acid or alkaline

Soil Quality

- The capacity of a soil to function to sustain biological productivity, maintain environmental quality and promote plant, animal and human health. Some indicators of soil quality include:

  - o Provides physical stability for plants.

  - o Accepts, holds and releases water to plants, streams and groundwater.

- Filters, buffers, degrades and detoxifies organic and inorganic materials.

- Promotes good root growth and maintains good biotic habitat for soil organisms.

- Stores and cycles nutrients and carbon.

- Maintains good soil structure to provide adequate aeration; also allows for rapid water infiltration.

- Moderate pH (~6.0–7.0) at which most essential soil nutrients are available.

- Low salinity levels.

- Low levels of potentially toxic elements (e.g., boron, manganese and aluminum).

Chapter
Resource

- Balanced fertility that provides adequate levels of nutrients plants and soil microbes require.

Plant Nutrients

- Sixteen essential nutrients required for plant growth – divided into four groups:

  1. Nonmineral - Carbon (C), Hydrogen (H), Oxygen (O)

  2. Macronutrients (primary elements) - Phosphorus (P), Potassium (K), Nitrogen (N)

  3. Secondary nutrients - Sulfur (S), Calcium (Ca), Magnesium (Mg)

  4. Micronutrients include: boron (B), chlorine (Cl), copper (Cu), iron (Fe), manganese (Mn), molybdenum (Mo), and zinc (Zn).

Plant Nutrients - Functions and Deficiencies

- Macronutrients and Secondary Nutrients

  - Nitrogen (N)

    ✓ Function: Promotes rapid vegetative growth and gives plants healthy green color; synthesis of amino acids and proteins.

    7

    N

    NITROGEN

    ✓ Deficiency signs: Stunted growth, pale yellowish color, spindly stalks; pale green color.

- o Phosphorus (P)

  - ✓ Function: Stimulates early growth and root formation; hastens maturity, promotes seed production; used in photosynthesis and respiration.

  - ✓ Deficiency signs: Purplish color in lower leaves and stems; dead spots on leaves and fruits.

- o Potassium (K)

  - ✓ Function: Improves plant's ability to resist disease and cold, stalk strength and seed quality.

  - ✓ Deficiency signs: Slow growth, margins on leaves develop a scorched effect starting on older leaves; weak stalk, shriveled seed or fruit.

- o Calcium (Ca)

  - ✓ Function: Aids in the movement of carbohydrates in plants; essential to cell wall division and root structure.

  - ✓ Deficiency signs: Terminal bud dies under severe deficiency; pale green color.

- o Magnesium (Mg)

  - ✓ Function: An ingredient of chlorophyll and enzymes; aids nutrient uptake.

  - ✓ Deficiency signs: Yellowing of leaves between veins starting with lower leaves, leaves abnormally thin, and tissues may dry and die.

- o Sulfur (S)

  - ✓ Function: Necessary for plant growth, root nodule formation; essential in amino acids.

  - ✓ Deficiency signs: Yellow upper leaves; stunted growth.

- • Micronutrients

o Boron (B)

   ✓ Function: Important to flowering, fruiting and cell division.

   ✓ Deficiency signs: Terminal buds die; thick, brittle upper leaves with curling.

o Copper (Cu)

   ✓ Function: Component of enzymes; chlorophyll synthesis and respiration.

   ✓ Deficiency signs: Terminal buds and leaves die; blue-green color.

o Manganese (Mn)

   ✓ Function: Chlorophyll synthesis.

   ✓ Deficiency signs: Dark green leaf veins; interveinal chlorosis.

o Zinc (Zn)

   ✓ Function: Needed for auxin and starch formation; active in many enzymatic reactions for plant growth.

   ✓ Deficiency signs: Interveinal chlorosis of upper leaves.

o Molybdenum (Mo)

   ✓ Function: Aids nitrogen fixation and protein.

   ✓ Deficiency signs: Stunted growth; pale green color.

o Chlorine (Cl)

   ✓ Function: Aids in root and shoot growth; deficiency is not seen in the field due to its universal presence in nature.

   ✓ Deficiency signs: Wilting, followed by chlorosis in leaves.

- o Iron (Fe)

    - ✓ Function: Essential for formation of chlorophyll, releases energy from sugars and starches.

    - ✓ Deficiency signs: Interveinal chlorosis of upper leaves.

| 26 |
| Fe |
| IRON |

Nutrient Availability and Interactions in Soil

- Plant nutrients must occur in the soil in available forms. They can be minerals, organic matter, adsorbed nutrients and dissolved ions.

- Factors of importance in nutrient interaction are soil pH and temperature, oxygen and water supply.

- Exchanges maintain the electrical balance of the root and soil

- Nutrient ions form when compounds dissolve in water.

    - o Charged atoms or molecules; a positive charge is a **cation** and a negative charge is an **anion**.

    - o Plant roots can absorb a nutrient ion, while soil particles adsorb ions.

- Nutrients may help or hinder the uptake of another nutrient. Examples include:

    - o Ammonium-potassium

    - o Potassium-magnesium

    - o Phosphorus-nitrogen

    - o Phosphorus-zinc

Chemical Properties

- Chemical properties of pH, cation exchange capacity, sodic, saline and organic matter relate to plant growth and availability of nutrients.

    - o Soil **pH**

        - ✓ Acidic – Having more hydrogen ions (pH of less than 7.0)

        - ✓ Alkaline – Having more hydrogen ions (pH of more than 7.0)

✓ pH of 7.0 is neutral

✓ Figure shows how pH affects the relative availability of micronutrients in soil

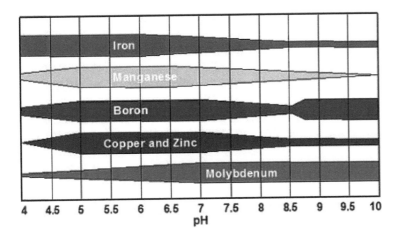

Chapter
Resource

o **Cation Exchange Capacity (CEC)**

✓ Ability of a soil to hold nutrients is directly related to the number of cations it can attract to soil colloids.

✓ Defined as the number of positive charges (cations) that a sample of soil can hold; expressed in terms of milligrams equivalents per 100 grams of soil and written as mEq/100g.

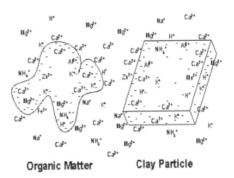

Organic Matter   Clay Particle

✓ This value, determined by the amount of clay, the type of clay, and the amount of humus, measured by cation exchange capacity (CEC) - expressed in milligram equivalents per 100 grams of soil (mEq/100 g).

✓ Organic matter and clay have a high mEq range and greatly influence the CEC.

✓ Soils that are highly weathered and have low organic matter have low CEC values.

✓ Clay soils with high CEC can retain large amounts of cations against potential loss by leaching.

✓ Percentage of the cation exchange sites filled with exchangeable bases is called the **base saturation,** an expression of how much of the soil's "potential fertility" the CEC, holds.

- ✓ Other cations are called **exchangeable bases** and include elements such as calcium (Ca), magnesium (Mg), potassium (K), and all plant nutrients except for sodium.

- ✓ **Exchangeable cations** are some cations not held very strongly and can be easily exchanged.

- ✓ Sandy soils with low CEC retain smaller quantities of cations.

- ✓ The opposite of cation exchange sites are anion exchange sites; anions are negatively charge ions; greatest in acid soils high in oxide clays.

○ Sodic and Saline Soils

- ✓ Contain excessive amounts of sodium (Na) with high pH values.

○ Saline-Sodic Soils

- ✓ Will also be saline (salty); characterized by Sodium (Na) saturation greater than 15% of CEC by pH of 8.4 or lower.

○ Organic matter

- ✓ Improves physical condition and structure

- ✓ Increases water infiltration

- ✓ Decreases erosion losses

- ✓ Supplies plant nutrients

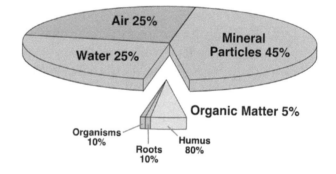

- ✓ Benefits from products released as organic residues decompose becoming available to plants over time.

- ✓ Serves as storehouse for reserve nitrogen (N).

- ✓ Maintained when sufficient crop residues returned to the soil.

○ CEC determines how agronomists use the soil:

- ✓ Clay soils measure high in CEC

- ✓ Sandy soils have low CEC

- ✓ Physical properties of soil are reflected in CEC

✓ CEC determines herbicide levels used in soils

✓ Liming of soils is determined by CEC

✓ Fertilization practices are determined by CEC

Soil Colloids

- **Soil colloids** are tiny clay and humus particles carrying a slight electrical charge which attracts nutrient ions. Silicate clays, oxide clays and humus are three types of soil colloids.

  o The electrical charge is negative which attracts cations from the soil; clays have different sites for negative charges making their capacity to hold cations different.

  o Negative charge of soil colloids plays a key role in the way nutrients behave in soil.

  o Nutrients are adsorbed on soil colloids.

    ✓ **Adsorption** is a surface function where plants take nutrients out of the soil solution and store the nutrients.

  o Silicate Clays

    ✓ A particle of silicate clay is called a **micelle**.

      ▪ Flat, plate-like crystal of many layers

      ▪ Each layer contains two or three sheets

      ▪ Sheets composed of silicon (Si), oxygen (O) and aluminum (Al)

      ▪ Clay types result from how layers are bonded together.

      ▪ Clays highly charged hold cations well; others are not.

      ▪ Clays can be sticky, plastic, or some swell when wet.

      ▪ If layers separate easily, water enters the micelle between the layers and the particle will swell when wet and shrink when dry.

      ▪ More surface area is exposed for adsorption of cations when layers separate

    ✓ More nutrients are contained in clays with loosely bound layers.

✓ Types of silicate clays include: mica clays, smectite clays, chlorite clays and kaolinite clays.

- Mica clays result from the weathering of mica minerals.

- Smectite clays are sticky and highly expanding

- In chlorite clays the layers are tightly bound by a fourth clay sheet.

- Kaolinite clays are used for making pottery as they swell the least and have the smallest surface area for the adsorption of soil cations.

o Oxide Clays

✓ Acts like sand; called sesquioxides; contain very small particles of iron and aluminum oxides; form stacked sheets but not like silicate clays; do not swell; not sticky; limited ability to hold nutrients.

o Humus

✓ Does not have physical properties of clays; ability to adsorb nutrients better than clay; not stable and will decay; not crystalline in shape.

Summary

Several factors are necessary for soil to supply nutrients for good plant growth such as sufficient minerals, nutrient rich, organic matter, pH balance, structure, adequate microorganisms and topsoil. Factors that affect soil fertility are the cation exchange capacity, uptake of nutrients, soil features such as temperature, pathogens, oxygen and water supply and water temperature. Good soil quality provides many functions to support good plant growth. Sixteen essential nutrients are required for good plant growth. These are divided into four groups – nonmineral, macronutrients, secondary nutrients and micronutrients. Each nutrient has a specific function in relation to optimum plant growth. These nutrients must occur in the soil in available forms along with soil pH, temperature, oxygen and water supply. Nutrient interactions maintain the electrical balance of the root and the soil for proper uptake. The chemical properties of soil pH, cation exchange capacity, sodic and organic matter relate to proper plant growth and the availability of the nutrients. Soil colloids are important because they carry a slight electrical charge which attracts nutrient ions. Nutrients are adsorbed on soil colloids. Adsorption is a surface function where plants take in nutrients from the soil. Different types of soil colloids are silicate clays, oxide clays and humus.

Additional Resources

Eash, N., C.J. Green, A. Razvi, W.F. Bennett and M. Bratz. 2015. Soil science simplified. 6th ed. Hoboken, NJ: Wiley-Blackwell.

Havlink, J.L., S.L. Tisdale, W.L. Nelson and J.D. Beaton. 2013. Soil fertility and fertilizers. 8th ed. Upper Saddle River, NJ: Prentice Hall.

Parker, R.O. 2010. Plant & soil science: Fundamentals and applications. Clifton Park, NJ: Delmar, Cengage Learning.

Soil and Water Conservation Society
http://www.swcs.org/

Soil Science Society of America
https://www.soils.org/

National Resources Conservation Service
http://www.nrcs.usda.gov/

Assessment

Take the online assessment here: https://goo.gl/FGTBBo
Download and print the expanded written assessment by scanning this QR code or by going to this URL: https://www.tagmydoc.com/Ch10SS

11 Soil pH and Salinity

Major Concept

Soil pH and salinity directly affect the ability of plants to absorb nutrients and water.

Objectives

- Define soil pH
- Name three factors in the development of soil pH
- List four common classes of soil pH
- Identify four problems with high acid soil
- Identify how pH affects plant growth
- Name steps to lime or acidify soil
- List how to treat saline and sodic soils
- Define salinization
- Name four ways to manage or treat salted soils

Key Terms

- Acid (soil)
- Alkaline (soil)
- Buffering capacity
- Burned lime
- Calcareous soils
- Liming
- Logarithmic scale
- Pelletized lime
- pH
- Saline soil
- Saline-sodic soil
- Salinization
- Sodic soils
- Sodium adsorption ratio

Chapter Resource

 Complementary *full color* illustrations, photos, charts and graphs are available by scanning this QR code or by following this URL: https://www.tagmydoc.com/SS11 These digital resources will enhance your understanding of the chapter concepts.

Soil pH

- Knowing a soil's pH can provide important information in diagnosing many soil problems because it affects the soil's biological, chemical and physical properties and processes, thereby affecting plant growth.

- Plant nutrition, growth and overall yields increase when pH is at an optimum level for a crop.

- Soil **pH** is a measure of acidity or alkalinity which affects the availability of nutrients for uptake by plants.

    o A soil's pH level influences biological activities and most chemical transformations in the soil.

    o Methods are available to bring the pH level to the desired range for a particular crop. For example, to raise the pH, lime is added; to lower the pH, sulfur is added.

- pH Scale

    o Soils contain both acids and bases (alkaline). The relative amounts of each are expressed by pH.

    o The pH scale ranges from 0 to 14.

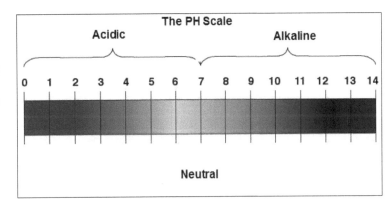

The PH Scale

Acidic   Alkaline

0 1 2 3 4 5 6 7 8 9 10 11 12 13 14

Neutral

    ✓ Soils with values below 7.0 contain more acids than bases and are referred to as acid or sour.

    ✓ Those with values above 7.0 contain more bases than acids and are referred to as alkaline or sweet.

    ✓ At 7.0, soil is neutral and contains equal amounts of acids and bases.

    ✓ The balance between hydrogen and hydroxyl ions determines pH level.

        ▪ Cation: hydrogen ion – solution acid

        ▪ Anion: hydroxyl ion – solution basic

    ✓ **Logarithmic Scale** – pH is measured on a logarithmic scale. This means a change of just a few pH units can induce significant changes in the chemical environment and sensitive biological processes. For example, a pH of 6 is ten times more acid than a pH of 7.

- Nutrient availability

    o Nutrients are most readily available to plants at a pH level between 6.0 and 7.0 with some plants having soil pH requirements above or below this range.

- o Soil pH is one of the most important soil properties that affect the availability of nutrients.

  - ✓ Macronutrients tend to be less available in soils with low pH.

  - ✓ Micronutrients tend to be less available in soils with high pH.

  - ✓ Soils that have a pH below 5.5 generally have a low availability of calcium, magnesium, and phosphorus. At these low pH's, the solubility of aluminum, iron, and boron is high; and low for molybdenum.

  - ✓ At a pH of 7.8 or more, calcium and magnesium are abundant. Molybdenum is also available if it is present in the soil minerals. High pH soils may have an inadequate availability of iron, manganese, copper, zinc, and especially of phosphorus and boron.

  - ✓ Many soil elements change form as a result of reactions in the soil which are controlled by pH, alter the solubility, and therefore, the availability, of nutrients.

- Toxicity – Soil pH controls the solubility and mobility of heavy metals, such as aluminum, iron, manganese, copper, zinc and nutrients, such as phosphorus.

  - o At low pH, particularly below 5.5, aluminum and manganese can reach toxic levels in the soil.

  - o Aluminum toxicity also increases water stress during dry periods because of poor root growth.

  - o Addition of fertilizer alters pH – Nitrogen fertilizers and manures either contain ammonium or cause ammonium to form in the soil, increasing soil acidity.

  - o As ammonium is converted to nitrate in the soil (nitrification), hydrogen ions are released; nitrates can combine with calcium, magnesium, and potassium and leach from the topsoil into the subsoil.

Development of Soil pH

- Typically soil pH levels range from 5.0 to 8.0 and are determined by many different sources.

- Naturally, pH is affected by mineralogy, climate, cation exchange, and weathering. Artificially, pH is altered during the process of managing soils. For example: Acid-forming nitrogen fertilizers or removal of bases (potassium, calcium, and magnesium).

Chapter
Resource

- Soil pH is dependent on temperature and moisture conditions and varies by regions.

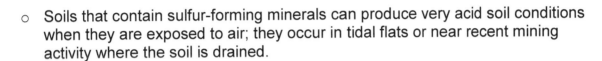

- Other factors to consider

  - Soil pH generally is recorded as a range in values for the soil depth selected.

  - Because pH is a measure of the hydrogen ion activity [H+], many different chemical reactions can affect it.

  - Soils that contain sulfur-forming minerals can produce very acid soil conditions when they are exposed to air; they occur in tidal flats or near recent mining activity where the soil is drained.

  - Tillage practices or continuous cultivation can change soil's pH.

  - Leguminous crops can slightly acidify soil.

    - ✓ Crops of soybeans, alfalfa, and clovers typically take up more cations than anions; causing hydrogen ions to be released from plant roots, resulting in soil acidification.

  - Young soils that have never experienced weathering or leaching will reflect the pH of their parent materials.

- How to know soil pH

  - Soil test results indicate when a soil is too acid or too alkaline. The pH of a soil should always be tested *before* making management decisions that depend on the soil pH.

    - ✓ A variety of kits and devices are available to determine the pH in the field. The methods include:

      - Colorimetric Method – Requires the use of colorimetric indicators. This method is widely used in the field, because it is simple and accurate enough for most purposes. The dyes change color with an increase or decrease of pH, making it possible to estimate the approximate hydrogen ion concentration of a solution. The soil sample is saturated with a dye. After a few minutes, a drop of the liquid is color compared to a chart to determine the pH.

- Electrometric Method – The hydrogen concentration of the soil solution is measured with an electrode specific for hydrogen ions. This instrument gives very consistent results but requires a skilled technician.

High and Low pH

- The most common classes of soil pH include:

Extremely acid	3.5 – 4.4
Very strongly acid	4.5 – 5.0
Strongly acid	5.1 – 5.5
Moderately acid	5.6 – 6.0
Slightly acid	6.1 – 6.5
Neutral	6.6 – 7.3
Slightly alkaline	7.4 – 7.8
Moderately alkaline	7.9 – 8.4
Strongly alkaline	8.5 – 9.0

- **Acid soils**: A low pH is caused by the percolation of mildly acidic water; exchangeable bases are replaced by hydrogen ions.

- **Alkaline soils**: A high pH is caused by reaction of water and the bases: calcium, magnesium, sodium, to form hydroxyl ions.

Acid Soils

- Soils become acidic when basic elements such as calcium, magnesium, sodium and potassium held by soil colloids are replaced by hydrogen ions.

- **Soil acidity** is a natural or induced chemical condition and can:

  - Decrease availability of essential nutrients

  - Decrease plant production and water use

  - Increase impact of toxic elements

  - Affect essential biological functions that occur in the soil (i.e.: nitrogen fixation)

  - Cause vulnerability in the soil structure leading to erosion

- If not corrected, soil acidification can have a major negative impact on agricultural productivity extending into subsoil layers causing problems to plant root development.

- Different causes of acidity:

  - Removal of plant material removes alkalinity, increasing soil acidity.

  - Rainfall, when precipitation exceeds evapotranspiration

  - Leaching of nitrate from soil

  - Adding nitrogen based fertilizer

  - Young soils that share the acidity of their parent materials: granite, sandstone, or shale

- Subsoil acidity - Even if the top 6 inches of soil show a pH above 6.0, the subsoil may be extremely acidic. If the soil pH is extremely acidic (below 5.2), lime should be applied early in the fall and turned as deeply as possible.

Alkaline Soils

- Soils formed under low rainfall conditions tend to be **basic** (alkaline) with soil pH readings around 7.0.

- In dry regions, when there is little to no percolation – calcium, magnesium, or sodium is carried upward into the root zone via capillary movement and forms hydroxyl ions.

- Soils in a very high alkaline range that are 100% base-saturated and contain several percent or more of calcium carbonate are known as **calcareous soils.**

  - Calcareous soils will fizz when diluted hydrochloric acid is applied due to carbon dioxide given off from the reaction between the mineral and the acid; do not change until most of the calcium carbonate is removed.

  - Because phosphorus, iron, copper, and zinc are less available to plants in calcareous soils, nutrient deficiencies are often apparent.

Effects of pH on Plants

- Crops vary in that each will grow best in a pH range specific to the type of plant and type of soil.

  - Plants growing on mineral soils will do well at a pH range of 6 to 7.

  - For organic soils, crops will do well in range of 5.5 to 6.

Chapter Resource

- Some plants (blueberry, alfalfa) prefer an acid or slightly alkaline soil.

- Hydrogen and hydroxyl ions are not the only factor to aid in plant growth. Several soil conditions (still related to pH) are also important:

  - ✓ Nutrient availability

  - ✓ Buildup of aluminum or metals in the soil

  - ✓ Presence of soil microbes

- Change the plant to the soil:

  - ✓ Select crops that can tolerate the existing soil pH. Plant breeders create crop varieties that are specifically tolerant of poor pH conditions.

Liming Soil (Raising pH)

- **Liming soils** that are acidic is a long time agricultural practice involving adding finely ground limestone to the soil.

  - The reaction rate for limestone increases when soil temperatures are warm and soil moisture is high.

  - Reaction is faster if the limestone is more finely ground.

  - The amount of limestone to apply depends on the amount of organic matter and clay, as well as the pH.

  - Crops will not respond immediately.

  - Liming helps crops with nutrient uptake from fertilizers, removes aluminum toxicity and promotes organism activity.

  - Lime is also a fertilizer; some limestone contains magnesium, important to correcting acidic sandy soils.

- How Lime Works

  - Neutralizes soil in two ways:

    1. Calcium replaces hydrogen and aluminum ions on exchange sites by mass action, raising the percent base saturation.

    2. Converts hydrogen ions to water.

- o Cation Exchange Capacity

  - ✓ Cation Exchange Capacity (CEC) is the capacity of the adsorptive components of a soil to attract and exchange cations.

  - ✓ The larger the cation exchange capacity (CEC), the more hydrogen a soil can hold, and the more lime it needs.

- o **Buffering capacity** is the capacity of a soil to resist change in pH.

  - ✓ Clay and organic soils have a high buffer capacity.

  - ✓ Buffering capacity is an important soil property when estimating how much lime to apply.

- • Benefits of Liming

  - o Foundation of a good soil fertility program; it also:

    - ✓ Supplies essential plant nutrients, calcium and magnesium, if dolomitic lime is used.

    - ✓ Makes other essential nutrients more available

    - ✓ Prevents elements such as manganese and aluminum from being toxic to plant growth.

    - ✓ Changes fertilizer efficiency (see table below)

Limestone Increases Fertilizer Efficiency and Decreases Soil Acids				
Soil Acidity	**Nitrogen**	**Phosphate**	**Potash**	**Fertilizer Wasted**
Extremely Acid — 4.5 pH	30%	23%	33%	71.34%
Very Strong Acid — 5.0 pH	53%	34%	52%	53.67%
Strongly Acid — 5.5 pH	77%	48%	77%	32.69%
Medium Acid — 6.0 pH	89%	52%	100%	19.67%
Neutral — 7.0 pH	100%	100%	100%	00.0%

Chapter
Resource

- Liming Materials

  o Liming materials contain calcium and/or magnesium in forms, which when dissolved, will neutralize soil acidity. Note: Not all materials containing calcium and magnesium are capable of reducing soil acidity. For instance, gypsum ($CaSO_4$) contains Ca in appreciable amounts, but does not reduce soil acidity.

  o Types of Limestone:

    ✓ **Calcium Carbonate Equivalent (CCE)** Expression of the acid-neutralizing capacity of a carbonate rock relative to that of pure calcium carbonate

    ✓ Liming materials contain calcium and/or magnesium in forms, which when dissolved, will neutralize soil acidity. Types of limestone include:

Liming Material	Composition	Calcium Carbonate Equivalent (CCE)	Description
Calcitic Limestone	$CaCO_3$	85-100	Ground limestone, contains mostly calcium carbonate, generally has less than 1 to 6% magnesium, neutralizing value depends on its purity and fineness of grinding.
Dolomitic Limestone	$CaCO_3$; $MgCO_3$	95-108	Ground limestone, contains mixture of calcium carbonate and magnesium carbonate, neutralizing effect depends on its purity and fineness of grinding.
Oyster Shells	$CaCO_3$	90-110	Oyster shells and other seashells are largely calcium carbonate, make a satisfactory liming material when finely ground, composed of primarily calcium carbonate and contain little or no magnesium.
Marls	$CaCO_3$	50-90	Deposits of calcium carbonate mixed with clay and sand, neutralizing value dependent on the amount of impurities (mostly clay) they contain, usefulness dependent on their neutralizing value and the cost of processing, must be dried and pulverized before use, usually low in magnesium, reaction with soil equal to calcitic lime.
Hydrated Lime	$Ca(OH)_2$	120-135	Contains calcium hydroxide, sometimes called slaked or builder's lime, powdery, and quick-acting, neutralizing value ranges between 120 and 135 compared to pure calcium carbonate.
Basic Slag	$CaSiO_3$	50-70	Product of the basic open-hearth method of making steel, calcium contained is in the form of calcium silicate, reacts with soil acids in a manner similar to ground limestone, generally has smaller particles than agricultural lime, it tends to change soil pH more rapidly than conventional agricultural lime. It also contains P_2O_5 ranging from 2 to 6% and some micronutrients and magnesium.
Gypsum	$CaSO_4$	none	Does not change soil pH. Gypsum is a soil conditioner that may be used to correct aluminum problems in the subsurface soil layers.

- ✓ **Pelletized Lime** – Finely ground limestone, pelletized with the aid of clay or other type of synthetic binder.

    - ▪ Usually spread with conventional spinner fertilizer spreaders.

    - ▪ Should be allowed to react with rainfall or irrigation on the surface before mixing into the soil.

- ✓ **Burned lime**, or quicklime, is made by heating limestone; heat drives off carbon dioxide resulting in the lighter calcium oxide:

$$CaCO_3 \text{-----> } CaO + CO_2 \text{ (gas)}$$

    - ▪ Less of it has the same effect as a larger weight of ground limestone.

    - ▪ Reacts more quickly in the soil but is caustic and may cake during storage; costly, hard to handle.

Acidifying Soil (Lowering pH)

- When a soil is too alkaline, the pH must be lowered as these soils have low infiltration capacity, making cultivation difficult.

- Over-liming can cause alkaline soil. If the pH of the soil is adjusted too high, it can induce nutrient deficiencies (such as phosphorus and micronutrient deficiencies), as well as permit molybdenum toxicity.

- Amending Techniques

    - ○ Addition of acid peat moss; temporary solution, feasible for only small areas.

    - ○ Application of anhydrous ammonia as a nitrogen fertilizer.

    - ○ Adding chemicals or acidifying minerals

        - ✓ Iron sulfate, Pyrite, Calcium Chloride, Urea

        - ✓ Aluminum sulfate: Not typically used in agriculture due to high cost, more of it is needed to produce same effect as elemental sulfur.

        - ✓ Apply Elemental Sulfur

            - ▪ Applied and mixed into soil, combines with oxygen and water to form sulfuric acid.

            - ▪ This oxidation of sulfur is brought about by certain microorganisms.

- Sulfuric acid releases hydrogen ions resulting in a lowered pH.

- The finer the sulfur is ground, the more rapid the conversion to sulfate and dilute sulfuric acid (three to six weeks or longer).

- The more free calcium carbonate present and the more buffered the soil, the longer it will take to acidify the soil.

- More sulfur will be needed on soils with free carbonates present.

Approximate Amount of Elemental Sulfur Needed to Increase Acidity (Reduce pH) of a Carbonate-Free Soil

CHANGE IN PH DESIRED	POUNDS OF SULFUR PER ACRE		
	SAND	SILT LOAM	CLAY
8.5 to 6.5	2,000	2,500	3,000
8.0 to 6.5	1,200	1,500	2,000
7.5 to 6.5	500	800	1,000
7.0 to 6.5	100	150	300

- A soil pH that is more than about 8.0 is considered high for most crops and is often also calcareous.

  o Calcareous soils have a high content of calcium carbonate. The pH of these soils does not change until most of the calcium carbonate is removed.

  o Because phosphorus, iron, copper, and zinc are less available to plants in calcareous soils, nutrient deficiencies are often apparent.

  o One option is to add these nutrients back into the soil rather than try to lower the pH.

Soil Salinity

- **Salinization** is the process by which water-soluble salts accumulate in the soil.

  o Excess salts hinder crop growth by limiting their ability to take up water.

- Salinization may occur naturally or because of conditions resulting from management practices.

- Any process that affects the soil-water balance may affect the movement and accumulation of salts in the soil. For example: Processes such as: hydrology, climate, irrigation, drainage, plant cover, rooting characteristics and farming practices.

- Accumulation of soluble salts more common in arid areas.

- What causes salinization?

  - Salinization on the soil surface occurs where the following conditions occur together: Soluble salts (sulfates of sodium, calcium, and magnesium) + high water table + high rate of evaporation + low annual rainfall = salinization.

  - Soluble salts of concern in the soil are sulfates (SO_4^{-2}), bicarbonates (HCO_3), and chlorides (Cl^-) of the bases calcium, magnesium and sodium.

  - These soluble salts can come from parent materials, salty irrigation water or de-icing salts.

  - Salinity problems affect about 25% of irrigated lands in the United States.

- Sodium is often measured by the **sodium adsorption ratio (SAR)**.

  - SAR compares the concentration of sodium ions with the concentration of calcium and magnesium.

  - Sodic soil has an SAR greater than or equal to 13.

- Three types of soil salinity are saline, sodic and sodic-saline, each presenting specific problems:

  - **Saline Soils**

    - Contain soluble salts and impairs productivity of plants but does not contain an excess of exchangeable sodium.

    - The soluble salts that occur come indirectly from the weathering of minerals and from waters which carry salts from other locations.

    - The presence of these soluble salts (including sodium chloride and sodium sulfate) interferes with the absorption of needed nutrients and water from the soil.

✓ **Sodic Soils**

- Exchangeable sodium percentage (or sodium saturation) is 15 or more, and pH is in the range 8.5 to 10.0. If soluble salts are not present, but exchangeable sodium is, the soil can be called "sodic".

- Sodic soils contain sufficient exchangeable sodium to interfere with the growth of most plants.

- Sodium becomes dominant in the soil solution and replaces calcium and magnesium on the clay, forming alkali soils.

- Adsorbed sodium causes disintegration of the soil aggregates, disperses the soil particles and reduces the pore spaces.

- These conditions all make leaching difficult because the soil becomes almost impervious to water resulting in restricted root penetration and reduced aeration.

- Plant tissues can be injured if enough sodium is taken up into the plant.

✓ **Saline-Sodic Soils**

- If soluble salts are present along with exchangeable sodium, the soil can be called "saline-sodic".

- Physical structure of these soils is normal.

- With leaching of soluble calcium and magnesium leaving behind the sodium salts, soil can become sodic.

- Reclaiming salted soils

  o Use high quality water with good drainage to leach out salts.

  o Subsoiling methods to break up hardpans.

  o Organic mulches improve saline soils.

Chapter Resource

  o Sealed soil surfaces impede drainage so sodic soils cannot usually be reclaimed simply by leaching.

    ✓ Gypsum added to soil to remove sodium first; after dissolving, calcium replaces sodium on the cation exchange sites.

- ✓ Finely ground sulfur will add calcium indirectly on soil containing some lime ($CaCO_3$).

- ✓ Bacteria convert the sulfur to an acid, then acid forms and reacts with soil lime to make gypsum:

$$CaCO_3 + H_2SO_4 \text{ --------------> } CaSO_4 + H_2O + CO_2 \text{ (gas)}$$

  - Conversion process takes time, so some growers use sulfuric acid with care for quicker results.

- Ways to manage and prevent salted soils:

  - Raise salt-tolerant crops.

  - Adequate leveling to avoid low spots where salt can accumulate.

  - Proper drainage during field preparation.

  - Use high-quality irrigation water with no salt.

  - Keep the soil moist to dilute soil salts, lowering the effect of osmotic potential.

  - Leaching salts out of root zones by careful over-irrigation.

  - Manures, crop residues and green manures added to soil.

  - Avoid over-fertilization.

  - Crops planted on ridge shoulders in furrow-irrigated fields.

  - Use of drip irrigation.

- Options for disposal of salted water or reducing discharges from fields:

  - Water delivery systems improved to reduce seepage and evaporation.

  - Improvement of irrigation efficiency; such as surge irrigation and careful budgeting to reduce percolation and tail water losses.

  - Practice minimum leaching to carry salts below the root zone, but not into the drainage system.

  - Re-use salty water on salt-tolerant crops; for example, barley or sugar beets.

Summary

Soil pH affects the soil's biological, chemical and physical properties and processes, thereby affecting plant growth. Soil pH is a measure acidity or alkalinity which affects the availability of nutrient uptake by plants. Nutrients are most readily available at a pH level between 6.0 and 7.0. Naturally, pH is affected by mineralogy, climate, cation exchange and weathering. Soil test results indicate when a soil is too acid or alkaline. Several methods are available to determine soil pH. Different plants may require different pH levels for optimum growth. Soils can be limed to raise the pH or lowered by the addition of anhydrous ammonia. Soil salinity is a process where water-soluble salts accumulate in the soil. Sodic and saline-sodic soils also interfere with absorption of needed nutrients. High quality water, addition of organic matter, breaking up the soil are ways to improve these soils.

Additional Resources

Plaster, E.J. 2013. Soil science and management. 6th ed. Albany, NY: Delmar Publishers.

Department of Natural Resources and Environmental Sciences: Soil Quality for Environmental Health
http://soilquality.org/indicators/soil_ph.html

Soil and Water Conservation Society
http://www.swcs.org/

Soil Science Society of America
https://www.soils.org/

National Resources Conservation Service
http://soils.usda.gov/technical/nasis/

Assessment

Take the online assessment here: https://goo.gl/C4jg4C
Download and print the expanded written assessment by scanning this QR code or by going to this URL: https://www.tagmydoc.com/Ch11SS

12 Plant Nutrition

Major Concept

Plant growth and level of health is directly related to the availability of required essential nutrients.

Objectives

- Define three rules determining if an element is dependent on a proper combination of nutrients
- Name the three primary nutrients
- Name the three secondary nutrients
- Identify the three nutrients listed on a fertilizer tag
- Name five of the seven micronutrients
- List the nutrients not supplied by soil
- Identify three purposes for soil builders
- Define what nitrogen sources availability are based on
- Explain what is compost
- List three macronutrients and how they promote plant health
- List five micronutrients and how they promote plant health
- Identify three common deficiency signs of older plants
- Identify three common deficiency signs of younger plants

Key Terms

- Compost
- Legumes
- Macronutrients
- Micronutrients
- Mottled
- Necrotic
- Rosetting
- Slag
- Soluble

Chapter Resource

Complementary *full color* illustrations, photos, charts and graphs are available by scanning this QR code or by following this URL: https://www.tagmydoc.com/SS12 These digital resources will enhance your understanding of the chapter concepts.

Plant Nutrition

- Plant growth and reproduction is dependent on a proper combination of nutrients; many of these essential elements are the same as those required by livestock and humans.

- o Rules for determining if an element is essential are as follows:

    - ✓ A lack of the element stops a plant from completing growth or reproduction.

    - ✓ Element is directly involved in plant nutrition.

    - ✓ A shortage of the element can be corrected only by supplying that element.

Primary Nutrients

- Nutrients used in the largest quantities (and always listed in this order) are:

    - o Nitrogen (N)

    - o Phosphorus (P)

    - o Potassium (K)

        - ✓ A fertilizer tag that reads 10-20-10, indicates the percentage ratio of Nitrogen, Phosphorous and Potassium and are always in this order.

Secondary Nutrients

- Calcium (Ca)

- Magnesium (Mg)

- Sulfur (S)

    - o Required in smaller amounts than the primary nutrients.

Micronutrients

- Minute amounts of these seven essential elements are found in plants and soils, but their roles are critical for plant nutrition.

    1. Chlorine (Cl)

    2. Iron (Fe)

    3. Boron (B)

    4. Manganese (Mn)

5. Zinc (Zn)

6. Copper (Cu)

7. Molybdenum (Mo)

Nutrients not Supplied by Soil

- Carbon (C)

- Hydrogen (H)

- Oxygen (O)

  o Supplied by air and water

  o Used in the largest amounts

Essential Plant Nutrient Sources

- Fertilizers (commercial and organic)

- Soil builders

  o Legumes

  o Manures

  o Green manures

Chapter Resource

- Nitrogen sources based on availability in the soil:

  o Quickly available: Inorganic salts that are readily **soluble** (dissolve) in water; industrially produced from raw materials such as natural gas and minerals. Includes: Ammonium Sulfate, Ammonium Nitrate, Ammonium Phosphate, and Potassium Nitrate, Urea.

  o Slowly available: Releases slowly over time; does not go readily into solution in water; referred to as slow-release such as SCU (Sulfur-coated urea). Includes slowly soluble forms: UF (Urea Formaldehyde) and IBDU (Isobutylidene diurea).

- Natural organic types: Emphasizes rotation with leguminous cover crops and application of compost or manure.

  o Treated sewage sludge manures are produced from the treatment of wastewater.

- o **Compost** – Decomposed organic matter.

- o **Legumes** – Nitrogen fixing plants grown for seed value such as alfalfa and peanuts.

- Phosphorus Sources

  - o Rock phosphate (PO_4^{3-}), mined and ground before being treated with acid to form the two principal phosphorus sources.

    - ✓ Super phosphate ($CaH_4P_2O_8$), formed by treating rock phosphate with sulfuric acid.

    - ✓ Treble super phosphate Ca (H_2PO_4)$_2$$H_2O$, formed by treating rock phosphate with phosphoric acid.

    - ✓ Ammonium phosphate – produced by reacting anhydrous ammonia (NH_3) with phosphoric acid (H_3PO_4).

    - ✓ Organic phosphorus sources – bone meal (animal bones ground into powder), rock phosphate (PO_4^{3-}) and colloidal phosphate (a soft-rock phosphate).

    - ✓ **Slag** – Byproduct of steel manufacturing and valued as fertilizer in gardens and farms in some areas of the country because of the slowly-released phosphate content in phosphorus-containing slag, and its liming effect.

- Potassium Sources

  - o Potassium Chloride or Muriate of Potash (KCl) – processed from mined potassium salts.

  - o Sulfate of Potash (K_2SO_4) and Potassium chloride treated with sulfuric acid.

  - o Potassium Nitrate (KNO_3) – Potassium chloride treated with Nitric Acid.

  - o Organic Sources of Potassium include: greensand having a very slow K release rate; langbeinite (Potassium-magnesium sulfate); Sylvinite (Potassium Chloride) KCl is restricted in the USDA standards unless it is from a mined source (such as sylvinite) and undergoes no further processing.

Plant Elements and Metabolism: Functions and Deficiencies

- **Macronutrients** are chemical elements required in large amounts for plant growth and development.

- Nitrogen (N)

  - ✓ Promotes rapid vegetative growth and gives plants healthy green color.

  - ✓ Deficiency signs: Stunted growth, pale yellowish color, burning of tips and margins of leaves starting at bottom of plant.

- Phosphorus (P)

Chapter
Resource

  - ✓ Stimulates early growth and root formation, hastens maturity, promotes seed production, makes plants hardy.

  - ✓ Deficiency signs: Small growth especially in roots, spindly stalk, delayed maturity, purplish discoloration of leaves on certain plants, dying of tips of older leaves, poor fruit and seed development.

- Potassium (K)

✓ Improves plant's ability to resist disease and cold, aids in the production of carbohydrates.

✓ Deficiency signs: Slow growth, margins on leaves develop a scorched effect starting on older leaves, weak stalk, shriveled seed or fruit.

- Calcium (Ca)

  - ✓ Aids in the movement of carbohydrates in plants, essential to healthy cell walls and root structure.

  - ✓ Deficiency signs: Terminal bud dies under severe deficiency, margins of younger leaves scalloped, blossoms shed prematurely, weak stalk or stem structure.

- Magnesium (Mg)

  - ✓ An ingredient of chlorophyll. Aids in the translocation of starch within a plant, essential for formation of oils and fats.

  - ✓ Deficiency signs: Yellowing of leaves between veins starting with lower leaves, leaves abnormally thin, and tissues may dry and die, leaves have a tendency to curve upward.

- Sulfur (S)

  - ✓ Aids in the formation of oils and parts of the protein molecules.

✓ Deficiency signs: Young leaves light green to yellowish in color. In some plants, older tissue may be affected also. Small and spindly plants. Retarded growth rate and delayed maturity. Interveinal **chlorosis** (a yellow leaf with a network of dark green veins) on corn leaves.

- **Micronutrients** (required in small quantities)

  o Boron (B)

    ✓ Aids in the assimilation of calcium; amount required is extremely small.

    ✓ Deficiency signs: Death of terminal growth, causing lateral buds to develop and produce a "witches'-broom" effect. Thickened, curled, wilted and chlorotic (bleached) leaves. Soft or **necrotic** (dead) spots in fruit or tubers. Reduced flowering or improper pollination.

  o Copper (Cu)

    ✓ Promotes formation of Vitamin A, excess is very toxic.

    ✓ Deficiency signs: Stunted growth. Dieback of terminal shoots in trees. Poor pigmentation. Wilting and eventual death of leaf tips. Formation of gum pockets around central pith in oranges.

  o Manganese (Mn)

    ✓ Serves as an activator for enzymes in growth processes. Assists iron in chlorophyll formation. Generally required with zinc in foliar spraying of citrus.

    ✓ Deficiency signs: Interveinal (between veins) chlorosis of young leaves. Gradation of pale green coloration with darker color next to veins. No sharp distinction between veins and interveinal areas as with iron deficiency. Development of gray specks (oats) interveinal white streaks (wheat) or interveinal brown spots and streaks (barley).

  o Zinc (Zn)

    o An essential constituent of several important enzyme systems in plants. It controls the synthesis of indoleacetic acid, an important plant growth regulator. The micronutrient most often needed by western crops. Many tree crops, grapes, beans, onions, tomatoes, cotton, rice, and corn require zinc fertilization.

    ✓ Deficiency signs: Decrease in stem length and a **rosetting** (circular arrangement of leaves) of terminal leaves. Reduced fruit bud formation. **Mottled** (spotted or blotched) leaves (interveinal chlorosis). Dieback of twigs after first year. Striping or ringing on corn leaves.

- o Molybdenum (Mo)

  - ✓ Required by plants for use of nitrogen. Plants cannot transform nitrate nitrogen into amino acids without molybdenum. Legumes cannot fix atmospheric nitrogen symbiotically unless molybdenum is present.

  - ✓ Deficiency signs: Stunting and lack of vigor. This is similar to nitrogen deficiency due to the key role of molybdenum in nitrogen use by plants. Marginal scorching and cupping or rolling of leaves. "Whip-tail" of cauliflower. Yellow spotting in citrus.

- o Chlorine (Cl)

  - ✓ Required in photosynthetic reactions of plants. Deficiency is not seen in the field due to its universal presence in nature.

  - ✓ Deficiency signs: Wilting, followed by chlorosis. Excessive branching of lateral roots. Bronzing of leaves. Chlorosis and necrosis in tomatoes and barley.

  Chapter Resource

- o Iron (Fe)

  - ✓ Essential for formation of chlorophyll, releases energy from sugars and starches.

  - ✓ Deficiency signs: Leaves yellowish or whitish (young leaves first), veins green, affected leaves curl up.

Nutrient Deficiency Signs

- Older Leaves – Effects are mostly generalized over entire plant; lower leaves dry up and die.

  - o Nitrogen (N)

    - ✓ Plants light green, lower leaves yellow, drying to brown, stalks become short and slender.

  - o Phosphorus (P)

    - ✓ Plants dark green, often red or purple colors appear, lower leaves yellow, drying to dark green, stalks become short or slender.

    - ✓ Effects are mostly localized, mottling or chlorosis, lower leaves do not dry up but lose the normal green coloration of leaves, leaf margins cupped or tucked.

- Magnesium (Mg)

  - ✓ Leaves mottled or chlorotic, sometimes reddened, necrotic spots (the death of most or all of the cells or tissue due to disease), stalks slender.

- Potassium (K)

  - ✓ Mottled or chlorotic leaves, necrotic spots small and between veins or near leaf tips and margins, stalks slender.

- Zinc (Zn)

  - ✓ Necrotic spots large and general, eventually involving veins, leaves thick, stalks short.

- Young Leaves – Terminal buds die, distortion and necrosis of leaves occur.

  - Calcium (Ca)

    - ✓ Young leaves hooked, then die back at tips and margins.

  - Boron (B)

    - ✓ Young leaves light green at bases, die back from base, leaves twisted.

    - ✓ Terminal buds remain alive but chlorotic or wilted, without necrotic spots.

  - Copper (Cu)

    - ✓ Young leaves wilted, without chlorosis, stem tip weak.

    - ✓ Young leaves not wilted, chlorosis, occurs.

  - Manganese (Mn)

    - ✓ Small necrotic spots, veins remain green

  - Iron (Fe)

    - ✓ Veins remain green

  - Sulfur (S)

    - ✓ Veins become chlorotic

Summary

Plants require thirteen elements from the soil for maximum plant growth. Carbon, hydrogen and oxygen, also required, are acquired from air and water. These elements function in plant metabolism. Deficiencies of these elements produce identifiable symptoms in plants. Fertilizers applied to the soil provide essential elements when they are low or lacking. Macronutrients are required in large quantities. Micronutrients occur in very small amounts in soils and plants. There are many sources of essential plant nutrients such as: fertilizers (commercial and organic) and soil builders. Recognizing nutrient deficiency signs is helpful in identifying problems in plant nutrition.

Additional Resources

Eash, N., C.J. Green, A. Razvi, W.F. Bennett and M. Bratz. 2015. Soil science simplified. 6th ed. Hoboken, NJ: Wiley-Blackwell.

Parker, R. 2010. Plant and soil science: Fundamentals and applications. (pg. 133-143) Clifton Park, NY: Delmar Cengage Learning.

National Resources Conservation Service
http://www.nrcs.usda.gov/wps/portal/nrcs/site/national/home/

Plant Nutrients
http://www.ncagr.gov/cyber/kidswrld/plant/nutrient.htm

Recognizing Plant Nutrient Deficiencies
http://www.unce.unr.edu/publications/files/ho/2002/fs0265.pdf

Roles of the 16 Essential Nutrients In Crop Development
http://www.eldoradochemical.com/fertiliz1.htm

Assessment

Take the online assessment here: https://goo.gl/6NXQfS
Download and print the expanded written assessment by scanning this QR code or by going to this URL: https://www.tagmydoc.com/Ch12SS

13 Soil Sampling and Testing

Major Concept

Soil testing helps maintain proper soil nutrient levels for optimal crop production.

Objectives

- Define the difference between soil sampling and testing
- List four benefits of soil testing
- Name three parts of soil sampling guidelines
- Define site specific management for soil
- List three types of soil testing
- Name three parts of laboratory soil tests
- Name three ways of non-lab soil testing
- Define laboratory tissue testing and the two benefits
- Name three methods of non-lab tissue testing
- Define near-infrared spectroscopy (NIRS)

Key Terms

- Composite sample
- Near-infrared spectroscopy (NIRS)
- Plant tissue test
- Precision farming

- Site-specific management
- Soil sampling
- Soil test

Chapter Resources

Complementary *full color* illustrations, photos, charts and graphs are available by scanning this QR code or by following this URL: https://www.tagmydoc.com/SS13 These digital resources will enhance your understanding of the chapter concepts.

Soil Test

- Soil testing includes:

    1. **Soil sampling** – A sample of the soil to be tested is collected and sent to a testing center.

    2. Soil testing – A soil laboratory tests the sample and makes recommendations to the grower.

3. Recommendations are considered by growers.

-   A **soil test** is a chemical evaluation of the nutrient supplying capability of a soil at the time of sampling; measures a certain portion of the total nutrient content of the soil. Several types are available:

    o   Standard Nutrient Analysis – This test is suitable for most purposes. Samples are analyzed for soil pH, macro and micro nutrients, and estimated total soil lead. Soils are hand-textured, and a visual estimate of the organic matter content is made. Limestone and fertilizer recommendations are made based on results.

    o   Soil pH Only – Soil pH levels are measured, and a limestone or sulfur recommendation is made if necessary. Soil pH is included in the Standard Nutrient Analysis.

    o   Soil Organic Matter – The percentage of organic matter is determined by a procedure called loss on ignition. Interpretation is provided but recommendations are not made.

    o   Soil Textural Analysis – The actual percent of sand, silt, and clay is determined, and the soil is categorized using USDA classification. No recommendations are given.

    o   Soluble Salts – This test measures the amount of total soluble salts by electrical conductivity. An interpretation is provided.

    o   Saturated Media Analysis – This test is provided for soilless potting media only. It is not appropriate for mineral garden soils. Results include macro and micronutrients, soluble salts, media pH, and nitrate-N and ammonium-N levels.

    o   Nitrate Testing – Some labs offers agronomic and commercial vegetable growers a Pre-sidedress Soil Nitrate Test (PSNT) from June 1st to August 15th and a Cornstalk Tissue Test in the fall and winter.

    o   Soil tests provide the most accurate method for determining the amounts of lime and fertilizer to apply.

    o   A low soil-test value for a nutrient means the crop will be unable to obtain enough of that nutrient and the deficiency should be corrected by adding the nutrient as a fertilizer.

Soil Testing Benefits

-   Determines nutrient levels in the soil

-   Determines the pH levels (lime needs)

- Provides a decision-making tool to determine what nutrients to apply and how much

- Potential for higher yielding crops

- Potential for higher quality crops

- More efficient fertilizer use

Soil Sampling and Guidelines

- To ensure a good soil sample, the following should be considered:

  - Sample must reflect overall or average fertility of a field; several (10-20) samples taken throughout the field regardless of acreage using a systematic scheme.

  - Depth of sample depends on the crop and tillage depth.

    - ✓ Samples can be from 4 inches to 4 feet.

    - ✓ Mix samples from one field thoroughly and save some for a **composite sample**.

    - ✓ Deep soil sampling greatly improves nitrogen recommendations for irrigated crops.

  - Take samples before growing season; closer to planting season is best as there is less chance for changes to occur.

  - Testing frequency depends on the crop and how it is grown. For most annual farm crops, sampling every two or three years is usually adequate; changes in crop type or tillage methods may require soil testing.

  - Stainless steel soil-sampling (moisture probe) is recommended for obtaining soil samples.

    - ✓ Tools must be clean and rust free.

    - ✓ Collect samples in plastic or stainless-steel containers.

    - ✓ Do not use galvanized or brass equipment.

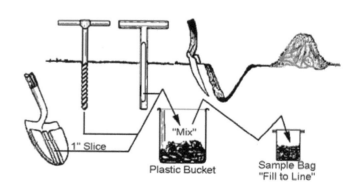

"Mix"

1" Slice

Plastic Bucket

Sample Bag
"Fill to Line"

- ✓ If using a shovel, make a V-shaped cut into the soil. Dig to the proper depth, removing a one-inch thick vertical slice up to the same depth from the smoothest side of the cut. From this sample, remove a one-inch strip of soil the length of the slice.

  o Samples should be air-dried within 12 hours to prevent microbes from mineralizing any organic matter.

  o Information forms should be filled out completely before mailing or taken to a laboratory; past crops grown, manuring, irrigation, etc., aids in the recommendation for fertilizer. County Extension or Cooperative Extension offices, agribusinesses, regional agronomists, or the Agronomic Division laboratory, are places soil samples can be mailed or taken for results.

- Greenhouse / container management

  o Potting mixes are used that have no access to reserve nutrients.

  o 100% of the nutrient level is created by the grower.

  o The management need increased by the small soil volume, high watering rates, and soluble salt problems of greenhouse plants.

  o Soils need to be tested before being transplanted to the field.

- Site-specific management

Chapter Resource

  o This is a kind of **precision farming** that involves very intensive and frequent soil testing and nutrient management. **Site-specific management** is individualized to small areas or "sites" to be tested and managed.

    ✓ Fields are divided into approximately sections and computers and other technology is used for ongoing testing and monitoring of soil fertility.

    ✓ Soil test results are entered into computer mapping software (GPS, GIS) and fertilizer needs are noted and applied accordingly.

Testing Options

- Soil tests performed in a lab generally analyze pH, nitrogen, phosphorus, potassium, calcium, magnesium, sodium, sulfur and salinity. More detailed tests are available which measure micronutrients such as zinc, iron, copper, manganese and boron.

- Types of Testing

o Visual inspection of crops for deficiency signs may uncover clear shortages. Method notes only critical shortages after yield damage has occurred. Visible symptoms may be unreliable.

o Soil tests measure nutrient levels in soil as well as other soil features such as lime and fertilizer needs. Soil tests cannot detect conditions that affect nutrient uptake, such as wet soils.

o Tissue testing measures nutrient levels in plant tissue itself. May uncover problems soil testing misses.

o Environmental tests – Some laboratories are now providing results relevant to environmental issues such as phosphorus loss from farming soils and heavy metal loading from waste application to soils. These tests are governed by state and federal regulations.

o A lab can perform a general analysis of soil or additional specific tests. Tests provided and those requested should be specific to the geographical area and crop type. Here is a guideline showing some general suggestions for selection of the proper soil test:

Routine Test: pH, Lime Requirement, Phosphorus (P), Potassium (K), Calcium (Ca), Magnesium (Mg), Manganese (Mn), Zinc (Zn)	Recommended for all commercial field and vegetable crops as well as lawns and gardens. Will give needed fertilizer and lime information.
Micronutrient Test Boron (B)	Helpful in cases of sandy or eroded soils low in organic matter. Crop types of: cotton, peanuts, alfalfa and vegetable crops.
Organic Matter Content	Applicable for all soils and crops, particularly helpful when tilth and water-holding capacity are important
Soluble Salts	For greenhouse beds, lawns. Not usually needed for field crops except in problem solving situation. Helpful if large quantities of fertilizers have been applied.
Nitrate Content (NO₃)	For field crop situations when pollution from fertilizer sources is a concern. As the residual NO_3-N level of a soil increases, the application rate of fertilizer nitrogen should be adjusted downward.
Commercial Greenhouse or Nursery Soil Test: pH, Soluble Salts, NH4, NO3, P, K, Ca, Mg	For mixes that include soil, sand, peat, pine bark, pearlite, and vermiculite used to produce greenhouse or potted vegetable, flower or ornamental plants. Not recommended for unamended soil.

- Laboratory testing

o Growers should use a local laboratory whose recommendations are based on local conditions.

o Labs will vary on what is tested in a general or standard series. This will all be noted on the soil testing form. Some tests performed will include:

✓ Evaluating the texture of the soil by manual or mechanical means.

✓ Measuring organic matter content by comparing the color of the soil sample.

✓ To determine liming application needs, pH is measured using a pH meter.

✓ Soluble phosphorous is measured by applying an acid solution to the soil sample and viewed using a spectrophotometer.

✓ Potassium is washed from the sample with a solution and its plant availability is measured.

o Once tests are complete, the lab will issue and mail a computer-generated report detailing all their findings.

o The Soil Test Report will include results, interpretation and recommendations. Typically, a column in the report will use terms like low or high to indicate how the numbers fall on a scale.

- Who Tests the Soil?

  o Cooperative Extension – Most land users will find that their local Cooperative Extension offices offer soil testing and recommendations in their laboratories at a very reasonable cost. Forms and boxes for soil sample may be available at a county Cooperative Extension center.

  o Commercial Labs – It is also an option to have soil tested at an independent lab. These can be found online or in local yellow pages. Private labs may offer additional tests, such as for pesticide or herbicide residue, nematode analysis and plant tissue analysis.

- How much does soil testing cost?

  o Cost vary depending on type of test and location. Some states offer tests for free or offer discounted rates during non-busy testing times. Some labs also give out gift certificates for lab tests. A more detailed soil analysis will cost more.

Name: Homeowner		Sample Date: April 9, 2007	
Lab Number: 12345		Your Sample Number: 1	
Crop to be Grown: Garden		Sampling Depth: 0 to 6 inches	
Soil Test Results		Interpretation	Recommendation
Nitrate-N	12 lb/acre	Low	3 lb N/1000 sq ft
	6 ppm		
Olsen Phosphorus	15 ppm	Medium	2 lb P_2O_5/1000 sq ft
Potassium	192 ppm	Medium	1 lb K_2O/1000 sq ft
Sulfate-S	15 ppm	High	————
Boron	0.5 ppm	Medium	0.02 lb B/1000 sq ft
Copper	1.7 ppm	Very High	————
Iron	47 ppm	Very High	————
Manganese	10 ppm	Very High	————
Zinc	1.3 ppm	High	————
Soluble Salts	0.3	Low	————
Organic Matter	3.4%	Medium	————
Soil pH	7.7	Medium/High	————
CEC	17.8	Medium	
Soil Texture	Sandy Loam		

Non-Lab Testing

- Relatively inexpensive, simple electronic devices such as digital pH meters, conductivity meters for measuring soil salinity and nutrient measuring devices are available for use in the field.

- Helpful in determining nitrogen needs of plants already in the growing season.

- Useful for greenhouse growers and container gardening that require constant monitoring.

- Some examples:

  - Testing Soil pH – Field test kits are available that test pH levels using color. Compact testing meters are also available for testing pH.

  - Preside-dressed NO_3^- test (PSNT) – Tests the soil for NO_3^- at early stages of plant growth and makes recommendations for side-dressing nitrogen (N) applications.

Plant Tissue Testing

- Plants themselves can be tested for nutrient content to determine fertilizer needs. Two types of **plant tissue tests**:

  - Rapid Tissue Testing – Green tissue is usually taken for this type of analysis. Chemicals are used to test the green tissue or the extract from the tissue. Not as accurate as dry tissue testing. Results should be verified using dry tissue testing.

Chapter
Resource

  - Dry Tissue Testing – This type of testing involves dried leaves or plants. The entire dried specimen is ground up and the total content of selected nutrients is determined. The plant part sampled, and stage of development is critical to interpretation of the results. Leaf analysis is time consuming and expensive compared to rapid tissue testing and soil analysis.

  - Plant tissue testing in combination with soil tests give the most complete picture of nutrient status.

  - Meaningful analyses require that the appropriate plant part be collected for the age of the plant and many plants must be included to obtain a representative sample.

Non-Lab Plant Tests

- Just as there are portable soil testing devices, several tests and kits can be used in the field with instant results.

- o Nitrate in Plant Tissue – A liquid color test using diphenylamine can be used on plant tissue to determine if additional nitrogen (N) is needed.

- o Plant Sap Test – Test kit that tests the plant for present nutrient levels. Parts of the leaf (petioles) are mixed with a liquid reagent in a vial or plant sap is squeezed onto test papers that have been pre-treated with the testing reagents.

- o Chlorophyll Content Meter – Detects nitrogen deficiency by shining a light through a leaf inserted into a slot on the device.

- o Chlorophyll Fluorometer – Measures variable fluorescence which indicates level of plant stress.

- o Leaf Area Meter – Monitors changes to leaf shape and size and stores data sets and digital images of the leaves in their memory.

Remote Sensing – Field Spectroscopy

- **Near-infrared spectroscopy** (NIRS) is a method that uses the near infrared region of the electromagnetic spectrum (from about 800 nm to 2500 nm). This method, typically used in the medical field, is now being used in soil analysis.

- A breakthrough in scientific studies has led to the use of visible-near infrared spectroscopy and remote sensing analysis to instantly assess soil properties and characterize soil nutrients.

- Coupling of this portable technology with remote sensing data, georeferenced ground surveys and new spatial statistical methods, has resulted in the capability for many samples covering a huge geographic area to be tested in real time with results comparative to a laboratory.

- These spectroscopes can also be used for assessment of water and nutrient levels in plant tissue.

Summary

Soil testing involves soil sampling and soil testing. Recommendations are given through laboratory reports. A soil test is a chemical evaluation of the nutrient supplying capability of a soil at the time of sampling and measures a certain portion of the total nutrient content. Besides determining the nutrient levels in the soil, testing provides a decision-making tool for growers to increase crop quality, yield and more efficient fertilizer use. Samples must reflect overall or average fertility of a field from 10 to 20 samples making a composite of a field. Precision or site-specific management uses GPS and GIS to manage an area of a field. Another method, which is relatively new, uses the near-infrared region of the electromagnetic spectrum (NIRS) to instantly assess soil profiles and characterize soil nutrients. These spectroscopes can also be used for assessment of water and nutrient levels in plant tissues. Generally, soil tests are performed in a laboratory, but growers can perform their own tests with purchased soil testing kits. Soil test reports from a laboratory will give interpretations and recommendations along with the results. Tissue testing can also be done using plants already in the growing phase. These reports, in combination with laboratory testing, give a complete picture of nutrient status.

Additional Resources

Crops and Soils Research for Soil Nutrients Analysis
http://www.asdi.com/applications/additional/agriculture-and-soils/crops-and-soils-research-for-soil-nutrients-analys

Soil Sampling and Testing
https://extension.purdue.edu/Marion/Pages/article.aspx?intItemID=4487

Collecting Soil Samples for Testing
http://www.hort.purdue.edu/ext/HO-71.pdf

Soil Sampling - University of Idaho Cooperative Extension System
http://www.cals.uidaho.edu/edcomm/pdf/EXT/EXT0704.pdf

New Mexico State University
http://articles.extension.org/pages/63494/soil-testing

Assessment

 Take the online assessment here: https://goo.gl/N4pkxa
Download and print the expanded written assessment by scanning this QR code or by going to this URL: https://www.tagmydoc.com/Ch13SS

14 Fertilizers

Major Concept

Fertilizers and fertilization of crops before, during and after the growing season is of major importance for crop success.

Objectives

- Define the purpose of fertilizer
- Name the four categories of fertilizers
- List the four forms of fertilizers for application
- Name and define the four types of fertilizer contents
- What does N, P, K mean on a fertilizer bag
- Explain the importance of fertilizer ratios
- Discuss how a soil test impacts fertilizer needs
- List three timing choices for fertilizing
- Name and define five ways fertilizer can be applied
- Discuss the effects of fertilizer on soil pH and salinity

Key Terms

- Banding
- Broadcasting
- Calcium carbonate equivalent
- Complete fertilizer
- Eutrophication
- Fertigation
- Fertilizer
- Fertilizer grade
- Fertilizer ratio
- Fillers
- Fluid fertilizer
- Foliar feed
- Granules
- Guaranteed analysis
- Hypoxia
- Mixed fertilizer
- Phosphorus index
- Pop-up fertilizer
- Pressurized liquid fertilizer
- Prills
- Pulverized fertilizer
- Side-dressing
- Slow-release fertilizer
- Soil injection
- Split application
- Starter fertilizer
- Straight fertilizer
- Topdressing

Chapter Resource

Complementary *full color* illustrations, photos, charts and graphs are available by scanning this QR code or by following this URL: https://www.tagmydoc.com/SS14 These digital resources will enhance your understanding of the chapter concepts.

What is Fertilizer?

- **Fertilizer** is a natural, manufactured or processed material or mixture of materials containing one or more of the essential nutrients; available in dry, liquid or gaseous form.

- Fertilizers enhance plant growth by adding nutrients into the soil and modifying the soil's ability of aeration and water retention.

Categories of Fertilizer

- Fertilizer can be grouped into four different categories: mineral, organic, synthetic organic and inorganic.

    o Mineral fertilizers are natural rocks and minerals rich in essential nutrients. The nutrients within mineral fertilizers are very slow to become available. The material must be ground very finely and is slow to dissolve. Some examples below:

Dolomite	Rich in calcium (Ca) and magnesium (Mg)	Used to raise the pH of acid soils
Langbeinite	Source of three essential nutrients: sulfur (S), potassium (K), and magnesium (Mg)	Used by eco-farmers in soil low in magnesium or potassium
Apatite (rock phosphate)	Rich source of phosphate (PO_4^{3-})	Phosphates are the naturally occurring form of the element phosphorus

    o Organic fertilizers are composed of organic materials, having some type of organic carbon (C) associated with them, and contain essential elements; contain the remains or a byproduct of a once living organism.

    ✓ Animal waste and manure are the most common examples.

    ✓ Peat, compost, food by-products, blood meal, crop residues, cover crops and sewage sludge are other examples. Note: Peat offers no value in terms of nutrition to the soil, but helps with aeration and water absorption.

    ✓ Some organic materials, particularly composted manures, and sludge, are sold as soil conditioners.

    ✓ Organic fertilizers usually contain fewer nutrients than inorganic sources, but are appealing in terms of cost and reusing environmental waste products.

    ✓ They also perform important functions which their synthetic counterparts do not: Increase organic matter content, increase bacterial and fungal activity, and improve the physical structure of the soil.

- ✓ Nutrients are released slowly over the growing season as the organic matter decays; therefore, organic fertilizers are considered "slow release" fertilizers.

- o Synthetic organic fertilizers are manufactured by industry. They are an organic substance chemically created from inorganic materials.

  - ✓ Synthetic organic fertilizers contain carbon (C)

  - ✓ Synthetic organic fertilizers contain carbon (C) and hydrogen (H).

  - ✓ An example of a synthetic organic fertilizer is the chemical synthesis of urea; fast acting and readily available to plants.

  - ✓ Other synthetic fertilizers, mostly urea derivatives, are made to be slow-release.

  - ✓ Nutrient content in synthetic fertilizers is generally high compared to mineral or natural organic fertilizers.

- o Inorganic fertilizers are manufactured or mined and are chemically inorganic.

  - ✓ Some inorganic fertilizers are manufactured by using high temperature and pressure to chemically reduce the original materials.

  - ✓ Most of these types of fertilizers dissolve quickly in the soil for rapid growth response.

Fertilizer Forms

- Fertilizers are provided or applied in many forms, giving growers several choices of application methods – divided into four main groups: pressurized liquids, fluid fertilizers, dry fertilizers and slow-release fertilizers.

  - o **Pressurized liquids** – Fertilizers held in pressurized tanks until they can be injected into the soil.

    - ✓ Anhydrous ammonia (NH_3) (one nitrogen and three hydrogen atoms) is injected directly into the ground where the ammonia converts to ammonium, providing nitrogen to plants. Ammonia is a gas at normal temperatures and pressure, but changes to a liquid when cooled to -28°F.

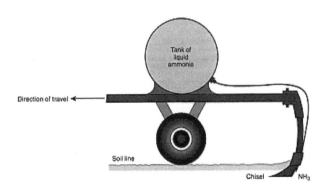

✓ Can be stored in large, high-pressure or refrigerated tanks; smaller tanks filled from storage tanks and pulled behind equipment to the field to be injected into the soil.

✓ The ammonia has been purified to contain no water. To remain in liquid form, it must be stored under high pressure.

o **Fluid fertilizers** are concentrated fertilizers that must be diluted with water; available in liquid form, powder, or pellets.

Chapter
Resource

✓ This category also includes suspensions which are made by combining a finely ground concentrated fertilizer with clay and then mixing with water.

✓ Fluid fertilizers are popular due to ease of use. They are easy to apply via several different methods and can be mixed with fluid lime or other chemicals.

o Dry fertilizers are applied to the soil and release nutrients after they have dissolved in water present in the soil. Types of dry fertilizers include:

✓ **Pulverized fertilizers** – Finely crushed powder, difficult to spread evenly, may cake during storage.

✓ **Granules** – Treated, evenly sized grains, spread evenly and easily, coated to reduce moisture absorption during storage.

✓ **Prills** – Free of dust, smooth, round, easy to use and spread, coated to protect during storage.

o **Slow-release fertilizers** are designed to slowly release nutrients into the soil over many weeks or even months.

✓ Slow-release fertilizers provide plants with a balance of nutrients throughout the life of the plant.

✓ Designed of materials that dissolve slowly; granular materials with membranes of resin or sulfur.

✓ More expensive than other fertilizers, but less overall application is used, and less leaching loss is experienced.

Fertilizer Contents

• Several types of fertilizer contents are: straight fertilizer, mixed fertilizer and complete fertilizer

- o **Straight fertilizer** – A fertilizer that contains only one nutrient.

  - ✓ Example: Ammonium Nitrate, which contains only nitrogen.

- o **Mixed fertilizer** – A fertilizer that contains two or more nutrients; may be created by mixing two different "straight" fertilizers together.

  - ✓ Example: Ammonium nitrate mixed with calcium phosphate to produce a new grade of fertilizer.

- o **Complete fertilizer** – A fertilizer that contains the three primary nutrients: Nitrogen (N), Phosphorus (P) and Potassium (K).

- • **Fertilizer analysis and grade**

  - o By law, all products sold as fertilizer require uniform labeling guaranteeing the minimum percentage of nutrients. Grade is often referred to as "N-P-K," which stands for nitrogen, phosphorus and potassium in that order. The three-number combination on the product identifies percentages of nitrogen (N), phosphate (P_2O_5) and potash (K_2O), respectively. For example, a 20-10-15 fertilizer contains 20% nitrogen, 10% phosphate and 5% potash. The product may also identify other nutrients, such as sulfur, iron and zinc if the manufacturer wants to guarantee the amount. This may be done by placing a fourth number on the product label and identifying what nutrient was added in the ingredients.

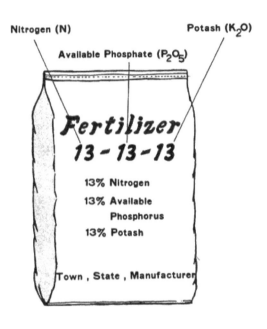

$$13\ N - 13\ P_2O_5 - 13\ K_2O = 1{-}1{-}1\ \text{Ratio}$$

  - ✓ A difference exists between the element form and the oxide form when looking at these elements. Phosphorus (P) and Potassium (K) are listed in their oxide form: phosphoric acid and potash which will have different measurements.

  - ✓ **Fillers** may be sand, clay granules, ground limestone or ground corncobs and are used to bring a load of bulk fertilizer to a weight of 1 ton.

  - ✓ Conditioners improve the quality of the fertilizer and make it easier to use.

  - ✓ **Guaranteed analysis** is the minimum amount of N, P_2O_5, K_2O, etc. in the fertilizer material. The Association of American Plant Food Control Officials

(AAPFCO) writes rules, definitions and labeling standards for the fertilizer industry. States then have laws for guaranteed analysis, sales and distribution.

- **Fertilizer ratio** indicates a comparative proportion of nitrogen to phosphate to potash. For example, a 15-10-5 fertilizer has a ratio of 3-2-1, and an 8-12-4 fertilizer has a ratio of 2-3-1. Fertilizer recommendations from a soil test are given in ratios.

  - ✓ Fertilizers can be custom blended to obtain the ratio that best suits the needs of the grower; necessary to determine how much of each carrier is needed to produce the final bulk blend.

Fertilizer Selection

- The soil test report indicates what nutrients the soil is lacking thereby allowing a better choice of a fertilizer or combination of fertilizers that will work best.

- Choose a compatible fertilizer for application choice; such as fertilizing with irrigation water, it must be water soluble.

- Growers choose which form (dry, liquid, etc.), based on cost and ease of use.

- Cost per pound of nitrogen (N), phosphorus (as P_2O_5), or potassium (as K_2O) is calculated using the total cost and the nutrient percentage in the fertilizer.

- Nitrogen: Nitrate or Ammonia

  - Nitrogen is the most frequently applied fertilizer; available in two forms: nitrate or ammonium or a mixture of the two.

    - ✓ Early-spring planting of cool-season crops: Nitrate

    - ✓ Fall fertilization, less nitrogen will leach out: Ammonia

    - ✓ Container plants, less root damage: Nitrate

    - ✓ Acid-loving plants: Ammonia

Fertilizer Application

- Nitrogen should be applied around the time crops are established.

- Phosphorous and potassium should be applied in the fall or spring, if needed.

- If micronutrients are to be added, they should be applied at time of planting.

- Limestone should be applied before crops are established.

- General or other needed fertilizers can be applied before crops are planted, during planting, mid-growth or all three.

  - Each timing choice has different advantages and disadvantages.

    - ✓ Pre-plant fertilizing will bring the soil's nutrient level up to a healthy level before crops are planted.

    - ✓ However, young seedlings may not receive needed phosphate as this nutrient does not move much in the soil.

    - ✓ Nitrogen may leach away before plants can use it.

    - ✓ Crops need nutrients during their growth for ongoing needs. This method is necessary for fertilization of perennial crops in the years after planting (i.e.: turf, orchards).

    - ✓ **Starter fertilizer** is a small quantity of fertilizer nutrients applied near the seed at planting which enhances the development of emerging seedlings by supplying essential nutrients in accessible locations near the roots.

    - ✓ Most post-plant fertilization focuses on renewing nitrogen during the growing season; most efficient time to apply nitrogen to rapidly growing crops.

    - ✓ **Split application**–Divide up the year's fertilizer needs into two or more parts and apply at each interval.

- Types of fertilizer application methods:

  Chapter Resource

  - **Broadcasting**–Fertilizer is spread uniformly over the field before planting; occurs by use of machinery or aircraft.

    - ✓ Fertilizer is left to filter into the soil on its own or is plowed into the soil using a cultivator.

    - ✓ Simple, economic method typically used on large fields.

  - **Soil injection**–Used to place liquid or gaseous fertilizer below the soil near the plants roots.

    - ✓ Also referred to as chiseling and can be used before crops are planted.

✓ Anhydrous ammonia can be injected using this method.

✓ Reduces losses through precise application of fertilizer.

○ **Banding**–Narrow bands of fertilizer are applied in furrows two inches from seeds or seeding and two inches deep.

   ✓ This method is used at the time seeds are planted and stimulates early plant growth and results in increased yields.

   ✓ Helpful method for no-till cropping systems where residues result in lower temperatures and higher moisture levels.

○ **Pop-up Fertilizers**–Also called seed placement, where a small amount of fertilizer is placed with the seeds during planting.

   ✓ Fertilizers applied using this method should have water-soluble complete fertilizers high in phosphate and have a low salt index (salt can damage seedlings).

   ✓ This method can be phytotoxic if too much fertilizer is used.

○ **Topdressing**–A type of surface broadcasting where fertilizer is spread over a growing crop and not mixed into the soil.

   ✓ High capacity spreaders can be used which spin dry fertilizer or spray liquid fertilizer on the crops.

   ✓ Method is fast and economical but may result in high nutrient losses.

○ **Side-dressing**–Fertilizer is applied to the soil six to eight inches from the plants along the rows.

   ✓ Used during early to mid-growth of a crop; used to supplement nitrogen needs and a popular method to apply split applications of fertilizer.

○ **Fertigation**–Fertilizer is added to irrigation water and applied to crops at intervals during the growing season.

   ✓ An injector draws concentrated fertilizer solution out of a tank and injects into the irrigation water, diluting to desired rate.

   ✓ Nitrogen (N) and Potassium (K) are sometimes applied with this method.

✓ A back-flow prevention system must be put in place to prevent fertilizer from being drawn back into the water supply; many states require a permit because of this danger.

○ **Foliar Feeding**—Nutrients are applied to the plant itself by using diluted fertilizer solutions that are sprayed on crop leaves.

✓ Nutrients applied this way are absorbed by the plant rapidly and effectively.

✓ Helpful when plants are lacking specific nutrients at a critical time, but should not be a substitute for soil fertilization methods.

Fertilizer Effects on Soil pH and Salinity

- Addition of fertilizer can sometimes significantly alter a soil's pH level and salinity.

  ○ There is a standard index for comparison of the acidity in different fertilizers. This standard is called the **Calcium Carbonate (CaCO₃) equivalent**. This index number is found on fertilizer labels and gives the number of pounds of Calcium Carbonate (CaCO₃) that would be required to neutralize a ton of the fertilizer in question.

  ○ Nitrogen is the main nutrient that will alter a soil's pH. Soils can become more acidic or alkaline depending on the type of nitrogen fertilizer used. Other forms of fertilizer can alter the soil's pH. This can be advantageous or detrimental depending on the starting level and the direction of change.

Chapter
Resource

  ○ Ammonium-based fertilizers will acidify the soil.

  ○ Anhydrous ammonia and urea have a lower potential for acidification.

  ○ If a fertilizer contains high amounts of potassium chloride or ammonium sulfate, this could lead to a potential salinity problem.

  ○ Soil must be hydrated and have proper drainage, so salt will not become concentrated.

Fertilizer and the Environment

- All fertilizers, manures or soil amendments need to be managed properly to reduce pollution and human health problems.

- Eutrophication and Hypoxia

○ Nutrient losses from farms and landscapes cause **eutrophication**–an increase of algae growth in water bodies. In many ecosystems; this is a slow, long term, but natural process.

✓ Fertilizer inputs dramatically speed up the process.

✓ The EPA rates eutrophication as the most widespread water-quality problem in the U.S.

○ In freshwater systems, while nitrogen contributes to the problem, phosphorus often limits algal growth and is a major cause of eutrophication in lakes and streams; may lead to loss of water quality, less dissolved oxygen in water and damaged ecosystems.

✓ Severe, extreme low-oxygen conditions, called **hypoxia**, results in major losses of aquatic life, including fish.

✓ Phosphorus enters surface waters primarily in runoff from fertilized or manured fields and lawns, either in solution or attached to soil particles.

nitrogen loading

nitrogen-rich surface water layers fuel algal blooms

algae bloom

algal cells die and decompose

decomposition lowers dissolved oxygen concentraitons in bottom waters

low dissolved oxygen stresses marine organisms

✓ Failure to incorporate manure leaves phosphorus to accumulate in the top couple inches of soil, where it can be removed by running water and transported into streams.

✓ **Phosphorus index,** quantifies potential phosphorus hazards on lands, to identify sites with a higher risk of phosphorus movement and to help devise corrective plans.

• Energy Cost

○ Fertilizers have a high energy cost, particularly nitrogen fertilizers.

○ Each ton of industrial fixed nitrogen consumes 1.5 tons of natural gas.

- Best Management Practices

  o Best Management Practices, or BMPs, are practical cropping systems that reduce environmental impacts of practices such as fertilization.

  o BMPs are used to maximize benefits of nutrients while minimizing the environmental impact, including not just fertilization and manuring, but irrigation and other practices, are included under the term nutrient management.

  o Estimates indicate, only half the Nitrogen applied to crops ends up on those crops – the rest is lost to water or the atmosphere.

  o Many practices described elsewhere are BMPs that improve nutrient use. Examples include:

Chapter Resource

    ✓ Conservation tillage that reduces erosion and runoff.

    ✓ Efficient irrigation practices that reduce nitrate leaching and denitrification on irrigated lands.

    ✓ Proper manure handling to increase nutrient retention and decrease leaching and runoff from feedlots and fields.

    ✓ Fertilization practices that deliver fertilizers at times and rates best suited to plant growth, such as split applications.

    ✓ Precise fertilizer applications resulting from good soil testing with credits taken for manure and legumes.

    ✓ Careful use of fertilizer on lawns and golf courses, such as sweeping up granules and clippings from sidewalks.

    ✓ Use of slow-release fertilizers and recycling of all irrigation water in container-growing nurseries and greenhouses.

    ✓ Controlled drainage systems.

    ✓ Vegetative buffers along sensitive areas.

    ✓ Cover cropping to take up excess nitrates before they can leach.

    ✓ Budgeting nutrient inputs so they equal nutrients removed by harvest.

Summary

Fertilization is important to crop growth and success. Fertilizer can be a natural or man-made material containing a single substance or a mixture of materials. Fertilizers are in four forms: pressurized liquids, fluid, dry and slow-release. Fertilizers can be grouped into four categories: mineral organic, synthetic organic and inorganic. Slow-release is more expensive but requires less overall applications. Fertilizer contents can contain only one ingredient or several depending on the crop and its needs. Fertilizer grades listed on a bag are N, P, K, along with some conditioners or fillers such as sand, clay granules and/or ground limestone to meet the weight requirements. Ratios may be necessary when comparing fertilizers. Soil test reports help to make determinations of the proper fertilizers needed for a crop. Fertilizers can be applied various ways and times depending on crop needs. Types of applications can be through broadcasting, soil injection, banding, pop-up fertilizers, topdressing, or sidedressing. Fertilizers can also be applied by irrigation water through the fertigation process. As nitrogen is the main ingredient in fertilization, this can affect the soil's pH and salinity. Fertilizers and any soil amendments need to be managed properly to reduce pollution and human health problems. Best Management Practices reduce environment impacts of fertilization practices.

Additional Resources

Environmental Protection Agency - Nutrient Management and Fertilizer
http://www2.epa.gov/agriculture/agriculture-nutrient-management-and-fertilizer

The Fertilizer Institute
https://www.tfi.org/

Assessment

Take the online assessment here: https://goo.gl/jajiCn
Download and print the expanded written assessment by scanning this QR code or by going to this URL: https://www.tagmydoc.com/Ch14SS

15 Organic Production

Major Concept

Organic crop production relies on many methods not used by traditional agriculture.

Objectives

- Define organic farming
- Define how sustainable agriculture is part of organic farming
- Identify four organic standards
- List three advantages and disadvantages of organic production
- Name four benefits of manure
- Define composting and give five benefits
- Define the process to create biosolids
- List four ways to organically control weeds
- Name four substances used as fertilizer for organic farming
- Name the two major water pollutants and three ways to reduce runoff waste
- Identify how best management practices help organic production
- Define sustainable agriculture

Key Terms

- Best Management Practices (BMP)
- Biosolids
- Composting
- Cover crop
- Crop rotation
- Cropping systems
- Green manure
- Organic farming
- Organic standards
- Sustainable agriculture

Chapter Resource

Complementary *full color* illustrations, photos, charts and graphs are available by scanning this QR code or by following this URL: https://www.tagmydoc.com/SS15 These digital resources will enhance your understanding of the chapter concepts.

Organic Farming

- **Organic Farming** is a farming method that involves growing and nurturing crops without the use of synthetic based fertilizers and pesticides. The Organic Foods

Production Act from the USDA defines the specific organic standards:

- o Preserve natural resources and biodiversity

- o Only use approved materials

- o Do not use genetically modified ingredients

- o Receive annual onsite inspections

- o Separate organic food from non-organic food

- From the USDA – *"Organic food is produced by farmers who emphasize the use of renewable resources and the conservation of soil and water to enhance environmental quality for future generations. Organic meat, poultry, eggs, and dairy products come from animals that are given no antibiotics or growth hormones. Organic food is produced without using most conventional pesticides; fertilizers made with synthetic ingredients or sewage sludge; bioengineering; or ionizing radiation. Before a product can be labeled "organic," a Government-approved certifier inspects the farm where the food is grown to make sure the farmer is following all the rules necessary to meet USDA organic standards. Companies that handle or process organic food before it gets to your local supermarket or restaurant must be certified, too."*

- Organic farming includes a measure of sustainable agriculture - The USDA Sustainable Agriculture website states *"Organic farming systems rely upon crop rotations, crop residues, animal manures, legumes, green manures, off-farm organic wastes, mechanical cultivation, mineral-bearing rocks, and aspects of biological pest control to maintain soil productivity and tilth, to supply plant nutrients and to control insects, weeds and other pests."*

- Rules are set for certain organic standards and prohibit the use of many substances on organic land including sewage sludge; a listing shows allowed and disallowed synthetic materials and labeling requirements.

- National and state standards define what can be sold as organic.

  - o Food to be sold as organic must bear a symbol that proves that it is truly organic.

  - o Symbol obtained through a certification organization.

  - o Complex procedure and is potentially expensive.

Organic Standards

- **Organic standards** are set by the USDA, Agricultural Marketing Service.

- Indicates the food or other agricultural product has been produced through approved methods.

- Specific requirements are verified by USDA-accredited certifying agents before labeled as USDA organic.

  - Organic regulations are the application of a set of cultural, biological, and mechanical practices that support the cycling of on-farm resources, promote ecological balance and conserve biodiversity.

  - Includes maintaining or enhancing soil and water quality, conserving wetlands, woodlands and wildlife.

  - Avoiding the use of synthetic fertilizers, sewage sludge, irradiation and genetic engineering.

- Sources of information are the Organic Food Production Act, USDA, and the National Organic Program.

  - The National Organic Program is within the AMS and develops the national standards for organically-produced agricultural products.

Advantages and Disadvantages of Organic Production

- Advantages

  - Different chemicals used as herbicides or pesticides

  - Lower input costs such as fertilizers

  - Higher prices received for products

  - Currently demand is greater than supply

- Disadvantages

  - More careful management required

  - No nutritional difference or added safety compared to conventionally grown products.

  - Higher production costs (management, labor)

- o Insect and disease pests can be more serious

- o Yields not consistent

- o Weed control is a challenge

Fertilizer for Organic Farming

- Organic farming relies mostly on the cycling of organic matter to maintain soil fertility.

  - o National Organic Program established standards for products labeled "organic."

  - o Substances used are compost, cover crops, plant by-products, animal manure, or other biological materials and mined minerals.

  - o Calculating how much nitrogen will be needed for a crop is an important consideration.

  - o Biosolids are allowed but not sewage sludge.

  - o Compost is defined in the regulation based on the carbon-to-carbon ratio, temperatures reached and duration.

  - o The Organic System Plan includes any fertilizers or amendments made.

  - o Recordkeeping for inputs of fertilizer are required

Animal Manure

- Application of manures at the proper time – using proper management techniques and in proper amounts:

  - o Recycles the nutrients through the soil profile.

  - o Reduces the expense of commercial (inorganic) fertilizers and the need to add organic matter.

  - o Improves water quality by preventing pollutants such as nutrients, organics and pathogens from migrating to surface and ground waters.

  - o Improves soil quality through addition of organic materials to improve soil tilth and increase water-holding capacity.

- o Air quality benefits from reduced emissions of methane and ammonia compounds and reduced odors.

- o Increases crop productivity

- Functions of manure management systems include:

  - o Production, collection, storage, treatment, transfer, utilization

- Manure management is complex because it also combines the physical aspects of rainfall, temperature, soil characteristics, or any constructed features, while working a management strategy to protect or enhance the ecological setting of the enterprise.

  - o BMP's for manure storage/handling include safe distances from streams and wells and flood plains, protected wellheads, store on soils with slow permeability areas, deep water tables and adequate storage capacity; test for nutrient levels; incorporate all manures into soil as soon as possible; consider composting or selling excess if no storage facilities.

- Contents of manure includes solid and liquid manure, which can include bedding/litter, wastewater (flush water or wash water), and spilled feed.

- Depending on the source of the manure, the inorganic contents are generally nitrogen, phosphorus, potassium and some zinc and sulfur.

- Under the Federal Clean Water Act of 1972, large feedlots can be considered point sources of water pollution, so their operations may be regulated.

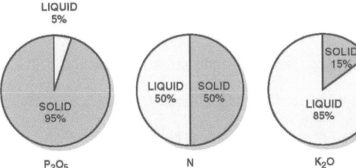

- A manure nutrient management plan helps in testing, in application rates, and in estimating nutrient availability.

- Actual composition of manures varies widely and should be measured.

- Table shows the sample nutrient composition of several manures, on an as-is basis (not dried or composted), in pounds nutrient per ton.

Pounds/Ton

Animal	N	P_2O_5	K_2O	S	Ca	Mg
Dairy Cattle	10	4	8	1	6	2
Beef Cattle	11	8	10	1	3	2
Poultry	23	11	10	3	36	6
Swine	10	3	8	3	11	2
Sheep	28	4	20	2	11	4
Horse	13	5	13	-	-	-

Composting

- **Composting** is the controlled biological decomposition of organic matter; sanitized through generation of heat; can be methodically done by close monitoring of measured inputs of water, air, carbon- or nitrogen-rich materials.

- Benefits of compost:

  o Enriches soil

  o Helps retain moisture

  o Suppresses plant diseases and pests

  o Reduces need for chemical fertilizers

  o Encourages beneficial bacteria and fungi

  o Reduces methane emissions from landfills

  o Reduces volume depending on aeration methods

  o Nitrogen reduction due to ammonia volatilization

  o Creates uniform particle size

  o Weed seeds destroyed

Biosolids

- **Biosolids** are nutrient-rich organic materials resulting from the treatment of domestic sewage in a treatment facility.

  - Biosolids go through physical, chemical and biological processes to clean the wastewater.

  - When treated and processed, biosolids can be recycled and applied as fertilizer; improve and maintain productive soils, stimulate plant growth, including timber growth; improves soil structure by increasing the soil's ability to absorb and store moisture.

  - Treated with lime to raise pH level to eliminate odors.

  - Sanitized to control pathogens or other organisms.

  Chapter Resource

  - Used by farmers and gardeners to promote growth of agricultural crops, fertilize gardens, parks and reclaim mining sites; occurs in all 50 states.

  - Reduces need for commercial fertilizers.

  - Biosolids can be used for composting.

  - Evaluation may be needed for application to a farm site; different rules for different classes of biosolids.

  - Nutrient management planning ensures quantity and quality are applied to farmland.

  - Nutrients found in biosolids, such as nitrogen, phosphorus and potassium and trace elements such as calcium, copper, iron, magnesium, manganese, sulfur and zinc, are necessary for crop production and growth.

  - Use of biosolids reduces the farmer's production costs and replenishes the organic matter that has been depleted over time.

  - Biosolids are available to anyone who complies with federal and state regulations.

  - Local governments now required to recycle biosolids as fertilizer, incinerate it or bury in a landfill.

Cover Crops/Green Manures

- Crops grown for a specific period and plowed under before maturing to improve soil fertility and quality; also called **green manures.**

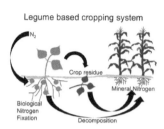

- Crops are generally a leguminous type; crop is grown to provide nitrogen for crop production; implemented as a conservation tool.

Choice of Crops

- Several factors are involved in organic crop selection:

  - Profitability

  - Suitability of soil

  - Water availability

  - Nutrient availability

  - Location, climate

  - Workforce availability

Crop Systems/Rotation

- **Cropping systems** are a total of all crops and the sequences and/or management practices used to grow those crops; proper soil management necessary to maintain or increase productivity of the crops.

  - Types of cropping systems include continuous cropping (monocropping), double cropping, intercropping, multiple cropping, rotation cropping, polyculture, relay intercropping, and strip cropping.

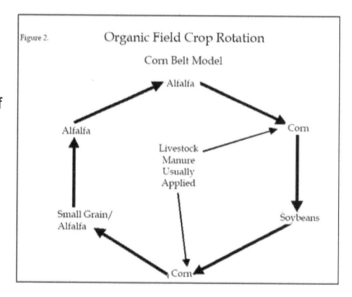

  - Soil conservation practices also include no- till, mulch-till, strip-till and ridge-till, contour cultivation and terracing.

  - **Crop rotation** is a systematic way to determine which crop to plant and when; builds soil fertility, aids in control of weeds, diseases and harmful insects.

Weed Control

- Ways to control weeds for organic production:

    o Diversify rotations; most effective means for keeping land weed-free.

    o Know the weed, their biology and ecology and where they are located.

    o Group crops with similar management.

    o Use the right tool for the system; mechanical versus mulch-type weed control; bed and row spacing of crop; combining of tools.

    o Cultural practices include preventing new weed species, prevent weed reproduction, match soil fertility with crop demand, let crop suppress weeds; use a calendar for timing effectiveness.

Use of Water for Organic Growing

- Major pollutants are nitrogen and phosphorous

    o Improper storage of compost and manure.

    o Exposure of waste to oxygen, nitrates, nitrites, phosphates form along with ammonia when nitrogen and hydrogen combine; these chemicals are carried to bodies of water by runoff through erosion and rain water.

    o Nutrient pollution is top cause of degradation in some U.S. waters; excess nitrogen and phosphorus lead to significant water quality problems including harmful algal blooms, hypoxia and declines in wildlife and their habitat; also leads to eutrophication or a decrease of dissolved oxygen in water.

- Ways to reducing runoff waste are:

    o Good nutrient management practices; slow-release forms of nutrients reduce risk of nutrient runoff and leaching.

    o Enhanced soil structure, water infiltration, and nutrient retention reduce risk of groundwater pollution.

    o Good management in respect to proper timing of crops, aeration of soils, use of vegetative buffers, use of manure fertilizers and appropriate time when crop can absorb them.

    o Infrastructure of farm, buildings should be considered.

Best Management Practice (BMP)

- Best Management Practice (BMP) means a practice, or combination of practices, that is determined to be an effective and practicable (including technological, economic, and institutional considerations) means of preventing or reducing the amount of pollution generated by nonpoint sources to a level compatible with water quality goals.

- BMP's should be a practical and affordable approach to conserve a farm's soil and water resources without sacrificing productivity.

    o From the USDA website: "*BMPs were developed and implemented as a requirement of the 1977 amendments to the Clean Water Act. BMPs are established soil conservation practices that also provide water quality benefits. They include such practices as cover crops, green manure crops, and strip-cropping to control erosion; and soil testing and targeting and timing of chemical applications (like IPM) to prevent the loss of nutrients and pesticides. District soil conservation agents use BMPs in helping individual farmers develop conservation plans for their farms.*"

Sustainable Agriculture

- The following statement is from the American Society of Agronomy in 1989 – "***Sustainable agriculture*** *over the long-term enhances environmental quality and the resource base on which agriculture depends; provides for basic human food and fiber needs; is economically viable; and enhances the quality of life for farmers and society as a whole.*"

    o Stability of the farm economy and community further motivate sustainable agriculture

    o Sustainable agriculture is a philosophy and collection of practices that seeks to protect resources while ensuring adequate productivity.

    o It strives to minimize off-farm inputs like fertilizers and pesticides and to maximize on-farm resources like nitrogen fixation by legumes. Top yields are less a goal than optimum and profitable yields based on reduced input costs.

    o Soil and water management are central components of sustainable agriculture. Techniques include crop rotation, conservation tillage, cover cropping and nutrient management.

    o Most of the goals of sustainable agriculture are common to all of modern agriculture.

Chapter
Resource

Summary

Organic farming is a type of sustainable farming that involves adhering to a strict set of standards prescribed by the USDA, Agricultural Marketing Service, and state and local entities. The organic symbol is earned through a certification process and is potentially expensive. The Nation Organic Program oversees this program also. There are many advantages and disadvantages of organic farming - expert management being crucial to making the venture successful. Organic farming uses animal manure, compost and biosolids. Careful management of these substances and adherence to the standards required is important to successful organic farming. Other considerations for farming organic are the type of cover crops or green manures used, the choice of crops, cropping systems and rotation of those crops, weed control, fertilizers and water type and availability. Best management practices help to make the enterprise successful. Sustainable agriculture principles aim to protect resources and maintain productivity – soil and water management being the main focus.

Additional Resources

Parker, R. 2010. Plant and soil science: Fundamentals and applications. (pgs. 220-236) Clifton Park, NY: Delmar Cengage Learning.

The National Organic Program (NOP) through the USDA AMS maintains a website:
http://www.ams.usda.gov/nop/NOP/NOPhome.html

USDA Climate Hubs
http://www.climatehubs.oce.usda.gov/content/environmental-benefits-organic-agriculture-water-quality

USDA Organic Agriculture
http://www.usda.gov/wps/portal/usda/usdahome?navid=organic-agriculture

EPA - Biosolids
https://www.epa.gov/biosolids

Sustainable Agriculture: Definitions and Terms
http://afsic.nal.usda.gov/sustainable-agriculture-definitions-and-terms-related-terms#termS7

Organic Farm Weed Management
http://extension.psu.edu/business/start-farming/vegetables/factsheets/creating-a-weed-management-plan-for-your-organic-farm

Assessment

 Take the online assessment here: https://goo.gl/uU15ic
Download and print the expanded written assessment by scanning this QR code or by going to this URL: https://www.tagmydoc.com/Ch15SS

Notes:

16 Tillage and Cropping Systems

Major Concept

Tillage and cropping systems differ according to the crop, soil conditions, economics, purpose and setting.

Objectives

- Define tillage and the reasons for tillage
- Describe the advantages and disadvantages of conventional tillage
- Describe the advantages and disadvantages of conservation tillage
- Name the two differences between primary and secondary tillage
- List the four general types of conservation tillage
- Define cropping systems
- List four cropping systems and describe them
- Identify some practices used in dryland farming
- Name four uses for rangeland

Key Terms

- Agro-forestry
- Allelopathy
- Conservation tillage
- Continuous cropping
- Conventional tillage
- Cover crop
- Crop rotation
- Cropping system
- Double cropping

- Dryland farming
- Fallow
- Green manure
- Intercropping
- Monocropping
- Mulch-till
- Multiple cropping
- No-till
- Polyculture

- Primary tillage
- Rangeland
- Relay intercropping
- Ridge-till
- Rotation cropping
- Secondary tillage
- Strip cropping
- Strip-till
- Tillage

Chapter Resource

Complementary *full color* illustrations, photos, charts and graphs are available by scanning this QR code or by following this URL: https://www.tagmydoc.com/SS16 These digital resources will enhance your understanding of the chapter concepts.

Tillage

- **Tillage** is preparation of the soil for a good seedbed growing environment

- Tillage purposes are to change the soil's physical conditions, for weed control, to incorporate nutrients and to control or manage crop residues.

- Tillage systems have changed over the years as new technologies have become available and the costs of fuel and labor have increased.

- Tillage systems can be rotated or varied to increase crop performance.

- Producers evaluate the need for tillage in each and every field to determine and improve profitability.

- Effects of tillage operations on the soil system and environment are also considered.

- Two types of tillage are: Conventional tillage and conservation tillage. Both have advantages and disadvantages.

  - **Conventional tillage** is a process of cultivating the soil to prepare a seedbed and for weed control. A sequence of events is used such as ploughing and harrowing and removal of plant residue from previous crops. Two types of tillage are primary and secondary.

    - ✓ **Primary tillage** initially breaks up the soil after a harvest to a depth of approximately 10-12 inches and buries residue from a previous crop.

    - ✓ **Secondary tillage** is not as deep as primary and creates a smoother finish to make a good seedbed.

    Crimped center disk blades

    - ✓ Different types of equipment are used for conventional tillage such as a lister plow, moldboard plow, chisel plow, harrow, disk or field cultivator.

    - ✓ Advantages of conventional tillage:

      - Loosen and aerates soil, aiding in planting the next crop

      - Destroys weeds and crop pests

      - Incorporates fertilizers

      - Dries soil before seeding for wetter climates

      - Creates good seedbed for better germination

✓ Disadvantages of conventional tillage:

- More trips across the field

- Dries the soil too much before planting

- Chemical runoff

- Reduces organic matter, microbes, soil aggregates creating potential for erosion

- Soil compaction

o **Conservation tillage** is a method that leaves the previous year's crop residue on a field from before and after planting a crop to reduce soil erosion and runoff.

✓ Approximately 30% of last year's crop residue on soil is considered conservation tillage.

✓ Can be used for almost any crop on any soil.

✓ Advantages of conservation tillage:

- Increased organic matter

- Increased water infiltration–cutting evaporation and runoff

- Increased earthworm population

- Reduced tilling time (trips across the field)

- Reduced erosion

✓ Disadvantages of conservation tillage:

- Surface and subsurface drainage may not be adequate.

- Crop diseases can remain in crop residues; biological or chemical application of pesticides, insecticides or fungicides, may be needed.

- Weed control may need to be addressed; careful application of herbicides considered.

- Special equipment needed to handle deep residue in relation to planting and fertilization

- Careful consideration of soil pH, lime and nitrogen due to additional surface residue.

✓ **No-till** is a way of growing crops or pasture from year to year without disturbing the soil through tillage; considered a type of conservation tillage; more many advantages than disadvantages.

✓ **Mulch-till** is a process where crop residue is spread uniformly over a field to aid in planting the next crop; accomplished by minimum tillage such as chiseling and disk harrowing to partially incorporate surface organic matter.

Chapter Resource

✓ **Strip-till** is the method of making narrow rows of 8 to 10 inches wide where seeds will be planted, leaving the soil in between the rows untilled; is considered a form of no-till; requires special equipment.

✓ **Ridge-till** maintaining ridges is essential; old residue removed into furrows in preparation for new crop; operating depth is shallow, disturbing only the ridge tops; some control of weeds and incorporation of herbicide possible.

o Other practices used with conservation tillage are contour farming, contour strip-cropping, contour buffer strips, terraces, grassed waterways or water and sediment control basins. (For details on these other conservation practices refer to Chapter 18.)

Cropping Systems

- **Cropping systems** are a total of all crops and the sequences and/or management practices used to grow those crops; proper soil management necessary to maintain or increase productivity of the crops.

- The interaction of plants with soil, soil organisms and crop pests are considered for even a simple crop rotation system.

- **Crop rotation** is a systematic way to determine which crop to plant and when; builds soil fertility, aids in control of weeds, diseases and harmful insects.

- Types of cropping systems depend on climate, grower preference, economics and market demand.

- Cropping systems include:

  o **Continuous cropping** or monocropping – The production of a single crop in a field.

- o **Double cropping** or sequential cropping – Planting a second crop immediately following the harvest of the first crop (also considered multiple cropping)

- o **Intercropping** or Relay cropping – Growing two or more generally dissimilar crops simultaneously on the same piece of land; grown in distinct rows.

- o **Multiple cropping** – Growing two or more crops consecutively or at the same time on the same field in the same year; crops needed that mature quickly to allow two harvests in one year.

- o **Rotation cropping** – A cropping sequence that includes more than one crop over several years.

- o **Strip cropping** – Growing soil-conserving and soil-depleting crops in alternate strips running perpendicular to the slope of the land

- o **Monocropping** or monoculture – production of a single crop in a field.

- o **Polyculture** – Growing multiple crops in the same space; includes multiple cropping, intercropping, companion planting, beneficial weeds and alley cropping; can imitate the diversity of natural ecosystems.

- o **Relay intercropping** – Growing two or more crops simultaneously during part of each crop's life cycle; second crop planted after first crop has reached reproductive stage of growth but before it is ready for harvest.

- • **Cover cropping** – planting used mainly to slow erosion and improve soil fertility.

  - o Referred to as **green manure** – crops grown for a specific period and plowed under before maturing to improve soil fertility and quality; generally, a leguminous type crop is grown to provide nitrogen for crop production; implemented as a conservation tool.

- • Considerations in any cropping system

  - o **Allelopathy** – a chemical substance released by one plant that can benefit or inhibit the growth of another plant.

  - o Uptake of nutrients is different for each crop rooting system.

  - o Crops differ in their water requirements.

- Mixed cropping systems can prevent or aid in spread of diseases and pests; some weeds may be beneficial or can be crowded out by the crop.

- Wise use of land and resources creates more stability and intensification in production of crops.

- **Agro-forestry** – A type of land management combining trees with agricultural crops and/or animals.

Dryland Farming

- **Dryland farming** is the profitable production of crops without irrigation or very limited, variable or unstable rainfall.

  - Crops can be cultivated during the dry part of the season from the stored moisture; 25% of rainfall on a fallow field will be stored for the following crop.

    - ✓ **Fallow** land is plowed land left without a crop growing for a season.

      - Potential problems: wind erosion; long-term decline in soil organic matter and quality; development of saline sweeps.

  - Dryland crops can include winter wheat, corn, beans, sorghum, sunflowers grapes, pumpkins or cotton depending on the season of year for rainfall.

  - Crops can be produced on as little as 9 inches of water per year.

  - Growers carefully evaluate potential yield throughout year for decreased or increased inputs of fertilizer or weed control efforts.

  - Drought-resistant and heat-stress tolerant crop varieties used.

Chapter
Resource

  - Good years of rainfall need to be capitalized on aggressively.

  - Erosion is a constant concern.

  - Wider rows for larger access to moisture for each plant.

  - Desert farming generally relies on water through drip irrigation or growing crops that are acclimated to desert conditions.

Rangeland

- **Rangelands** are those lands on which native vegetation is mostly grasses, grass-like plants, forbs (herbaceous flowering plant that is not a grass), or shrubs suitable for grazing or browsing; also includes woodlands and most deserts, shrublands, tundra, alpine communities, marshes and meadows.

  - Range and pasture lands are found in all 50 states; nearly half the land on earth is rangeland.

  - Provides forage for beef cattle, dairy cattle, sheep, goats, horses and other types of domestic livestock.

  - Primarily for livestock production but wildlife is also a major economic consideration – dependent on these lands for food and cover.

  - Grazing lands include grazed forest lands, grazed croplands, hayland and native/naturalized pasture.

  - Environmental values of rangeland is extensive and provides many essential ecosystem services such as clean water, wildlife and fish habitat and recreation uses, mineral/energy production, renewable energy and other natural resources; intangible benefits such as scenic, cultural and historical values; aesthetic and spiritual values are of great importance to quality of life.

Summary

Tillage is the preparation of the soil for a good seedbed growing environment. Tillage changes the soil's physical characteristics, is for weed control, to incorporate nutrients and manage crop residues. Tillage systems have changed over the years incorporating new technologies. The major types of tillage are conventional and conservation. Each has advantages and disadvantages. Different types of equipment are used for each type of tillage. There are many types of cropping systems for crop rotations. Each is determined by local weather and soil conditions, soil management, crop types, marketing demands, economics and space available. Dryland farming is farming with very limited water availability and needs to be managed carefully. Rangeland is used mainly for animal grazing and provides essential ecosystem services such as clean water and other natural resources, along with intangible benefits such as scenic, cultural and historical values.

Additional Resources

Parker, R.O. 2010. Plant & soil science, fundamentals and applications. Delmar Cengage Learning.

Plaster, E.J. 2013. Soil science & management. 6th ed. Delmar Cengage Learning.

Iowa State University Agronomy Extension, Soil Management/Environment, Tillage and cropping systems
http://www.agronext.iastate.edu/smse/tillage/

Penn State Extension, Cover crops for conservation tillage systems,
http://extension.psu.edu/plants/crops/soil-management/conservation-tillage/cover-crops-for-conservation-tillage-systems

https://www.agronomy.org/

http://www.sare.org/

http://www.nrcs.usda.gov/wps/portal/nrcs/detail/national/climatechange/?cid=stelprdb1077238

http://www.nrcs.usda.gov/wps/portal/nrcs/main/national/landuse/rangepasture/range/

http://www.nrcs.usda.gov/wps/portal/nrcs/detailfull/national/energy/conservation/?cid=nrcs143_023637

http://cropwatch.unl.edu/

Assessment

 Take the online assessment here: https://goo.gl/p1pK8g
Download and print the expanded written assessment by scanning this QR code or by going to this URL: https://www.tagmydoc.com/Ch16SS

17 Horticultural Uses of Soil

Major Concept

Horticultural uses of soil are many and varied and present many benefits and challenges.

Objectives

- Identify how horticulture differs from agriculture production
- List six vegetable crops
- Name five factors when considering vegetable production
- Define pomology and list seven considerations for this culture
- List three important considerations for nursery field culture of plants
- Identify eight challenges for container growing of crops
- List three of the five key elements in successful turf management
- Name the key components in landscaping success.
- Define xeriscaping

Key Terms

- Core aeration
- Landscaping
- Micro-irrigation
- Olericulture
- Penetrometer
- Perlite
- Pomology
- Vermiculite
- Vertical mulching
- Xeriscaping

Chapter Resource

Complementary *full color* illustrations, photos, charts and graphs are available by scanning this QR code or by following this URL: https://www.tagmydoc.com/SS17 These digital resources will enhance your understanding of the chapter concepts.

Horticulture Systems

- Horticulture systems incorporate both science and aesthetics. From the American Society of Horticulture Science *"Horticulture is the science and art of producing, improving, marketing, and using fruits, vegetables, flowers, and ornamental plants. Production and consumption of high quality fruits and vegetables allows us to maintain a healthy, balanced daily diet. Flowers and ornamental plants enrich our homes and communities, and contribute to our sense of well-being. Horticulture impacts our lives on a daily basis by providing nutritious fruits and vegetables, offering visual enjoyment, and promoting recreational activities."*

- Horticulture is part of agriculture. Many agricultural practices common to field crops apply to horticulture.

- The quality of soil is important for success for the home garden, small farm enterprises, to large agricultural/horticultural operations.

- There are many types of horticultural systems. A few listed here are:

  - Vegetable culture

  - Fruit culture

  - Nursery field culture

  - Container growing

  - Landscaping

Vegetable Culture

- Vegetable culture is also called **olericulture** and deals with non-woody plants for food.

- Vegetables are the most important horticultural crop in terms of total value and play a critical role in human nutrition.

- These crops generally include: root crops, bulb crops, salad crops, solanaceous (tomatoes, peppers) crops, sweet corn, cole (cabbage, cauliflower) crops, legumes, cucurbits (melons, squash, cucumber) crops, and greens (spinach, collards).

- Vegetables are grown the world over and transported to many places; China is the largest vegetable-producing nation.

- The production of vegetable crops also includes: cultivation, harvesting, storage, and preservation.

- Keys factors to consider for vegetable production are: Soil quality and health, site selection (physical characteristics as contour, soil depth, water and air drainage), water supply and quality, crop and variety selection and market development.

  - Most vegetables do well in well-drained, sandy loam.

  - Vegetable crops generally require more total water and more frequent irrigation than most other crops.

- Crop varieties and species that are disease-resistant increase chances for success.

- Marketing plans should be carefully considered because of the perishability of the product.

Fruit- and Nut-Culture

- Fruit- and nut-growing culture is also called **pomology** – the study and cultivation of fruits and nuts. Many of these are long-lived woody plants that remain in place for many years.

- Important considerations for the fruit- and nut-growing farmers are:

  - Well-drained, fertile soil

  - Soil acidity and fertility; soil testing recommendations; tissue testing to provide status of tree health

  - Rooting zone may be 2 feet deep

  - Air circulation, as cold air is heavier than warm air

  - Amount of sunlight available

  - Appropriate variety in area to be grown

  - Choice or availability of rootstock

Vineyard

  - Specific planting and spacing requirements

  - Control vegetation under trees and in rows through mulching, herbicides, light cultivation; cover crops in row middles a consideration

  - Control of insects and diseases through commercial pesticides or organic controls; sanitation important

  - Pest controls especially for long-term growth of trees

  - Fertilize with care; use recommended allowances from soil test

  - Training and pruning

Nursery Field Culture

- Nursery field culture is where and how plants are propagated and grown to a usable size usually in large, outdoor settings. Aspects of nursery field culture include site selection and preparation, seed or variety selection, management of soil and water, and fertilization.

  - Site selection and preparation includes soil that is well drained, loamy and pH of approximately 6.0, slightly sloped field is beneficial.

  - Seed selection is important for area, soil, and water requirements

  - Management of soil and water; irrigation systems vary depending on crop needs and location.

  - Fertilization – Soil testing to determine needs of crop, application of compost, animal manure or green manure, or commercial fertilizer applied

  - Cultural practices include weed control, irrigation, and pest and disease control

- Other aspects of nursery field culture are market opportunities and labor availability as this type of farming is labor-intensive work.

Container Growing

- Growing of plants in containers differs significantly from plants grown in the soil because of the limited soil, space, and nutrients.

Chapter Resource

- Challenges to growing container plants are:

  - Irrigation/fertilization/nutrients

    - ✓ Quality of water, testing for high levels of dissolved lime, particularly, bicarbonates

    - ✓ Timing of irrigation should be consistent; consideration of runoff water

    - ✓ Chemical properties of mixes are different and can change rapidly in response to watering and fertilization

    - ✓ Potting mixes lack colloids (substances which stay dispersed in solution) such as clay, so are poorly buffered (resisting pH change) against chemical change.

    - ✓ Soluble salts found in water, such as inorganic soil constituents (ions) build up to high levels in the mix.

✓ High-rates of fertilization with inadequate leaching easily damages plant roots.

✓ Needs of plants are specific and should be closely monitored

o Growing media

✓ Can be soil with added amendments; or soilless potting mixes which include coarse sand, **perlite** (large granules of light-weight expanded volcanic glass), **vermiculite** (expanded mica), shredded plastics or other materials

✓ Well-aerated mixes are important because of container space limitations

✓ Heat, steam or chemicals are used by green-house growers to sterilize or pasteurize soil-based mixes

✓ Strict sanitation and fungicides are also used to prevent infections by soil organisms.

✓ Soil temperature is a consideration especially when exposed to direct sunlight, wind or cold temperatures.

Turf Management

- The successful management of turf in any environment or for any use is dependent upon the interactions of soil, water, air, sunlight and fertilizer or nutrients.

  o Soil - Loams, sandy loams best; pH of 6.0; 4 – 6 inches depth; soil test to determine needs of soil; tilling to mix topsoil/subsoil and cut weed growth and break up soil; addition of new topsoil

    ✓ Perforating or aerating the soil with small holes to allow air, water, and nutrients to penetrate the grass/roots, reducing soil compaction and controlling thatch. **Core aeration** is mechanically removing plugs of soil and thatch from a lawn.

  o Water

    ✓ Water – pH should be 6.0 to 7.0; test to determine if there are any chemicals whether high or low; drainage issues addressed; water weekly to one inch if a new grass to build root system; water when cool

  o Fertilizer and nutrients

✓ Soil test to determine need for lime and fertilizer; starter fertilizer good; maintain nutrients to keep up with fast-growing grasses

Landscaping

- **Landscaping** is basically the care and maintenance of a landscape or ornamental plantings.

- A wide and varied types of landscaping depending on the use, setting, soils, water availability to name only a few.

- Landscaping designs are available to fit all scenarios from metropolitan or small town, mountains, desert or jungle.

- Landscapers are familiar with the soil, pH, water requirements and capacities of their region along with what grows well in a chosen area. Items of consideration for landscaping can include:

  o Soil surveys – A resource for help in determining soil properties and features, maps, boundaries or for placement of landscaping needs.

  o Salinity and pH measured with a soil test or portable testing devices; amending pH for plant needs.

    ✓ Acidification is common and can be done by adding sphagnum peat moss to the backfill. As the peat moss decays, the pH returns to normal.

    ✓ Many sources of lime raise the pH on a landscape site, including lime in a concrete foundation, limestone rock mulches and alkaline irrigation water.

    ✓ Annual use of acid-forming fertilizers such as ammonium sulfate or special acid preparations may maintain acidity.

    ✓ Sulfur-coated urea, a slow-release fertilizer, will also enhance acidity.

  o Compaction measured by a penetrometer; tillage may be recommended or **vertical mulching** to allow for movement of air and water in soil or devises used which inject air or water into compacted soil.

  o Soil color related to soil drainage; percolation testing

  o Transplanting techniques to encourage rapid root growth; mulches used that conserve moisture without depleting soil oxygen; fertilize carefully, especially trees.

- Xeriscaping

  - **Xeriscaping** is a type of landscaping that reduces or eliminates the use of water. Considerations for xeriscaping include:

    - ✓ Planning to determine use of xeriscaping is critical to success; placement according to exposure to sun; terracing or sloping considerations.

    - ✓ Soil preparation – soil that supports healthy plant life and conserves moisture has coarse soil clusters or aggregates, sand and pore spaces; may have as much as 50% by volume pore space; good balance of sand, silt and clay needed; organic matter added annually

    - ✓ Plant selection – plants that can survive under low-moisture conditions; withstand dryness or grow with little watering; spaced further apart for water demands.

    - ✓ Mulches can improve soil and reduce water use by decreasing soil temperature, and soil exposed to wind; organic mulches become part of the soil; can reduce weeds

  - Conserving irrigation water

    - ✓ Precision landscape irrigation minimizes water usage by replacing turf with woody and herbaceous plants that can tolerate **micro-irrigation** (low pressure/ low discharge) which lowers water usage, as does reducing plant populations.

    - ✓ Observe water coverage; some areas irrigated differently; coordinate landscape design with irrigation system

Summary

Horticultural systems incorporate both science and aesthetics. Horticulture differs from agriculture in that horticulture deals with fruits, vegetables and ornamentals while agriculture deals with field crops and animals (agronomy, crop science, plant science, animal science, etc.) Many types of horticultural systems exist, which can include vegetable culture, fruit culture, nursery culture, container growing and landscaping. Vegetable culture is also called olericulture. Vegetables are the most important horticultural crop in terms of total value. Fruit and nut culture is also called pomology. These are long-lived woody plants that remain in place for many years. Nursery field culture is planting and growing plants on a large scale to a usable size, usually in an outdoor setting. Container growing of plants requires close management because of limited space and soil. Successful turf management is dependent on the interactions of soil, water, air, sunlight and fertilizer. Landscaping is the care and maintenance of a landscape or ornamental planting in a variety of settings worldwide and requires knowledge of soil and water requirements. Xeriscaping is a type of landscaping requiring little or no water.

Additional Resources

Plaster, E.J. 2013. Soil science and management. 6th ed. Albany, NY: Delmar Cengage Learning.

Association of Professional Landscape Designers
https://www.apld.org/about-apld/

Arizona Cooperative Extension - Vegetable Garden: Container Garden
http://ag.arizona.edu/pubs/garden/mg/vegetable/container.html

Colorado State University – Xeriscaping: Creative Landscaping
http://extension.colostate.edu/topic-areas/yard-garden/xeriscaping-creative-landscaping-7-228/

Washington State University – Designing a field grown nursery
http://gardencenternursery.wsu.edu/inGround/DesigningFieldGrownNursery.htm

Assessment

 Take the online assessment here: https://goo.gl/XXVwwB
Download and print the expanded written assessment by scanning this QR code or by going to this URL: https://www.tagmydoc.com/Ch17SS

Notes:

18 Soil Erosion and Conservation

Major Concept

Soil erosion and conservation is preventing, slowing or stopping wind, water or soil movement.

Objectives

- List two types of soil erosion
- Identify the effects of soil erosion
- Name four consequences of erosion control
- Name three practices that contribute to erosion control
- Describe management practices that aid in erosion control
- Identify conservation tillage methods in controlling soil erosion

Key Terms

- Cover crop
- Crop rotation
- Cultivation on the contour

- Sod crops
- Soil erosion
- Strip cropping
- Terracing

- Tilth
- Water erosion
- Wind erosion

Chapter Resource

Complementary *full color* illustrations, photos, charts and graphs are available by scanning this QR code or by following this URL: https://www.tagmydoc.com/SS18 These digital resources will enhance your understanding of the chapter concepts.

Types of Erosion

- **Soil erosion** is the movement of soil particles from one place to another under the influence of water or wind

- **Water erosion** is caused by raindrops, surface flow and gully flow. A selective process in which organic matter and finer soil particles are removed first which rapidly destroys productivity of cultivated land.

  - Splashing of raindrops on bare loams, sands and sandy soils, separates organic matter, silt and clay from sand.

✓ These materials are then washed away by surface flow and the heavy sand is left on the field.

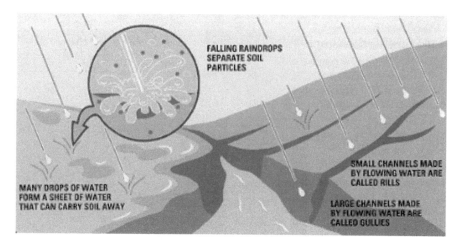

- This sand is turned under at the next plowing of the field or mixed with the surface layer of the soil at the next cultivation.

✓ In either case, a fresh supply of topsoil is brought to the surface for further action.

○ Repeating this procedure over the years produces a sandier soil, particularly in areas of severe erosion.

✓ Sandier soil is less able to hold moisture and nutrients, and is therefore less productive.

- **Wind erosion** is common in dry areas where soils are often bare of vegetation and high wind velocities are common.

○ Wind catches the lightweight silt and clay particles (organic matter) and blows them away, leaving behind sand and other coarse materials.

○ Organic matter, silt and clay, are the most important parts of the soil, because they supply the nutrients needed by plants.

✓ As the nutrient supply is reduced, crop production declines.

Cultural Practices Contributing to Soil Erosion

- Plowing land which is unsuitable for cultivated crops.

- Plowing soil in areas with too little rainfall to support continuous crop production.

- Breaking up large blocks of land susceptible to erosion.

- Failure to maintain crop residues on the surface while the soil is not protected by growing crops.

Chapter
Resource

- Exposing soil on slopes.

- Removing natural vegetation from forest lands.

- Reducing and weakening plant growth by overgrazing.

Consequences of Erosion

- Loss of the most essential part of the soil - the topsoil, with its finer soil particles, better **tilth** (ability to be worked), superior water-retention capacity, more plentiful mineral and organic elements and helpful bacteria.

- Reduction of crop yields

- Need for greater use of plant and commercial fertilizers

- Production of lower nutrients crops

- Formation of gullies, by which erosion is speeded and farmland made impossible to cultivate

- Covering of rich bottomlands by soils from poorer highlands

- Destruction of road banks and removal of bridges

- Erosion by stream banks of valuable bottomlands

- Silting of ditches, streams, dams, lakes and reservoirs

- Increased flood hazard because of more rapid runoff

- Waste of water that could be used for farming and other purposes

- Greater costs for production resulting in higher prices for consumers

Soil Conservation Practices

- No-till

  o Planting with no prior tillage

o Seed is placed in a slot formed by the planter and weed control is achieved entirely by surface application and contact herbicides.

- When managed properly, no-till production works well on many soils.

- Use of thick-growing **sod crops** that cover the ground surface and fill the surface soil with fibrous roots tend to hold the soil in place and reduce erosion.

- **Strip cropping** is the practice of planting two crops in alternating strips or alternately planting a strip and leaving a strip fallow on land that would otherwise be erodible.

   o Usually a cultivated crop is alternated with non-cultivated crops. The strips should be planted on the lines of contour.

   o **Cultivation on the contour** is the practice of planting and cultivating of crops following the contours of the land.

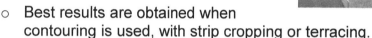

   o Effective water erosion control can seldom be obtained from contour cultivation alone.

   o Best results are obtained when contouring is used, with strip cropping or terracing.

- Terraces to remove runoff safely

   o **Terracing** is the practice of constructing embankments or ridges across sloping soils.

   o Main reason for terracing in wet areas is to construct a ridge across a slope to guide surplus water off a field at an angle rather than straight down the hill.

   o In dryland areas, terraces are constructed to increase water penetration, and reduce runoff, that is the water is "held" on the terrace rather than flowing down the hill as runoff

- Use of crop rotation

   o **Crop rotation** is the growing of selected crops in a regular order on any field.

- Principle objectives of a good rotation are to secure more economical and more consistent production of crops over a period of years and to control soil erosion.

- **Cover crops**

  - Green cover protects soil during fall, winter and early spring when most prone to erosion.

  - Cover crops are plowed down the following spring.

    ✓ Winter rye and other winter crops work well for this purpose.

Chapter Resource

- Building of ponds and dams

  - Artificial ponds hold or impound water which, otherwise, would be lost as runoff, carrying soil with it.

Summary

Soil erosion is the movement of soil particles from one place to another under the influence of water or wind. Erosion by water is caused by raindrops, surface flow and gully flow. Erosion by wind is common in dry areas where soils are often bare of vegetation and high wind velocities are common. Cultural practices that contribute to soil erosion are plowing land unsuitable for crops, not maintaining crop residues on soil surface, removing natural vegetation and over grazing. Several soil conservation practices are used to control soil erosion, such as thick-growing sod crops to cover the ground surface, cultivating on the contour, strip cropping, terracing, the use of crop rotation, no-till techniques, cover crops and building ponds and dams.

Additional Resources

Parker, R. 2010. Plant and soil science: Fundamentals and applications. Clifton Park, NY: Delmar Cengage Learning. (Pg. 155-163)

Natural Resource Conservation Service – Conservation Practices
http://www.nrcs.usda.gov/wps/portal/nrcs/detailfull/national/home/?cid=nrcs143_026849

Plant & Soil Sciences eLibrary
http://passel.unl.edu/pages/index2col.php?category=soilscience

Assessment

Take the online assessment here: https://goo.gl/MBGttE
Download and print the expanded written assessment by scanning this QR code or by going to this URL: https://www.tagmydoc.com/Ch18SS

Notes:

19 Urban Soil

Major Concept

Urban soils need to be studied and managed differently because they are generally found in populated areas.

Objectives

- List four points concerning urban soils and their composition
- Name three characteristics of urban soils
- List the four processes that affect soil in urban settings
- Name three ways to avoid compaction
- Define a brownfield
- List four ways to create or modify soil
- Identify four ways erosion can be controlled in an urban setting
- Name three options for zero-runoff

Key Terms

- Bioremediation
- Bioswales
- Brownfield
- Hydrophobic
- Hydroseeding
- Recharge basins
- Retention ponds

Chapter Resource

 Complementary *full color* illustrations, photos, charts and graphs are available by scanning this QR code or by following this URL: https://www.tagmydoc.com/SS19 These digital resources will enhance your understanding of the chapter concepts.

Urban Soils

- In populated areas

- Used for plant growth

- Less favorable from natural soils

- Found in parks, recreation areas, community gardens, green belts, lawns

- Increasing with population and in developed areas

- Urban Soil Characteristics

  - Varies throughout landscape and in vertical soil profile.

  - Changed through movement and compaction by storage of soil, aeration or water drainage.

  - Various items added through human intervention such as solid and chemical contaminants.

  - pH changes due to buried concrete and other contaminants.

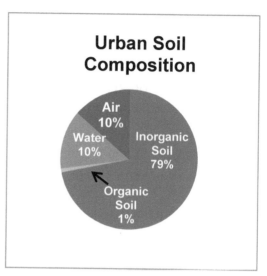

Urban Soil Composition

- Contamination through disruption of nutrient and organic matter cycling.

- Soil temperatures higher from "heat island" effect of urban areas.

- Soils repel water instead of absorbing – **hydrophobic**.

Variabilities in Soils

- Many processes in urban settings can affect soil such as:

  - Cut and fill operations, buried debris, compaction and contamination

    - ✓ Cut and fill operations change soil over a small area

    - ✓ Buried debris can be any variety of items such as masonry scraps, wood, or any rubble and prevents or causes excessive drainage of water; prevents root growth; raises pH; soil may be difficult to work.

    - ✓ Compaction may include heavy equipment or simply cars parked on a construction. Other problems can be:

      - Vibrations of nearby roadways

      - Uncontrolled vehicle or foot traffic

      - Sensitive trees and plants can be affected or difficulty in establishing landscaping, turf; growth of weeds which are compaction-tolerant

- Increased erosion

- Compaction measured by bulk density; when bulk density rises above 1.4 g/cm^3, root growth begins to suffer from lack of air and direct physical resistance.

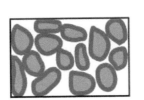

Soil Particles
Water
Air

Non-compacted   Compacted

- Bulk density of 1.7 g/cm^3: roots cannot penetrate the soil; table indicates bulk density relationships based on soil texture:

Soil Texture	Ideal bulk densities for plant growth (grams/cm^3)	Bulk densities that affect root growth (grams/cm^3)	Bulk densities that restrict root growth (grams/cm^3)
Sands, loamy sands	<1.60	1.69	>1.80
Sandy loam, loams	<1.40	1.63	>1.80
Sandy clay loams, clay loams	<1.40	1.60	>1.75
Silts, silt loams	<1.40	1.60	>1.75
Silt loams, silty clay loams	<1.40	1.55	>1.65
Sandy clays, silty clays, clay loams	<1.10	1.49	>1.58
Clays (> 45% clay)	<1.10	1.39	>1.47

- Compaction avoided by proper planning; breaking up compaction, deep tillage, amendments, increased organic matter, special pavers, aerating machines

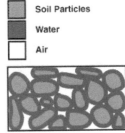

Core aerator

✓ Soil contamination impacts usability and can include contaminants; may require reclamation. Included are:

- Heavy-metals such as lead contamination are toxic to children and occur in urban areas; toxic to plant roots

- Soils should be tested, and amendments mixed in, including inorganic materials

- **Brownfields**

  - Defined by the EPA "*With certain legal exclusions and additions, the term '**brownfield site**' means real property, the expansion, redevelopment, or reuse of which may be complicated by the presence or potential presence of a hazardous substance, pollutant, or contaminant*".

  The EPA's Brownfields Program creates many benefits for local communities.

  - Cleaning up and reinvesting in these properties protects the environment, reduces blight, and takes development pressures off greenspaces and working lands.

  - Historical records, soil and site assessments help to determine renovation strategies.

- Site planning can include **bioremediation**—the use of living things to reduce pollution; seeding with soil bacteria to break down organic pollutants

  - Phytoremediation is an innovative use of green plants to clean up the environment. The term comes from the Greek word for plants ("phyto-") that can detoxify, or remediate, soil or water contaminated with heavy metals or excess minerals.

- Modified and Structured Soils

  - Use of existing soil or creating new soil with additional amendments

  - Organic amendments added each season

  - Using A and B soil horizons to create new soil

  - Hard compaction broken up but slight compaction for unforeseen settling

  - Structured soils are very different from standing soils

  - Contain crushed stone mixed with clay loam and polymers to hold water and bind mixture

  - Requirement met for load-bearing pavement

  - Space for air exchange for root growth

Chapter Resource

Urban Soil Erosion and Control

- Erosion many times greater during construction

- Subsoil may be exposed which can erode more easily

- Newly graded areas creating additional runoff need to be addressed so roads and foundations are not damaged.

- Planning using soil surveys and topographic maps

- Ways to keep erosion, runoff and sedimentation regulated:

  o Retain natural soil cover as much as possible

  o Keep changed areas small and protect them

  o Reduce runoff and keep away from changed areas

  o Maintain sediment on-site by using silt fences, debris basins and **retention ponds** (manmade depressions installed to collect runoff water).

- Vegetation

  o Native plants and grasses planted properly

  o Use permanent turf where mowing is not a problem

  o Divert runoff before planting

  o Soil worked through and any amendments added

  o Erosion controlled

  o For slopes or steep areas, use **hydroseeding**, a mixture of water, seed and shopped straw; can also be sodded

  o Universal Soil Loss Equation (USLE) is a widely used mathematical model to identify soil erosion; used to estimate average annual soil loss.

- Urban Zero-Runoff Options

  o Rapid removal of storm water

  o Landscape graded to move water to storm sewers or culverts; reduces flooding in developed sites.

- ✓ Grading may move flooding downstream, carrying pollutants and sediments to streams and rivers, reducing groundwater recharge.

- ✓ Areas graded to retain water for soil filtration

- o Runoff water can be used as irrigation and a recharge source

- o Keeping water on-site:

    - ✓ For lawns and other vegetation to absorb water.

    - ✓ Porous concrete for parking lots and sidewalks

    - ✓ Retaining on-site wetlands or creating new ones.

    - ✓ **Recharge basins** – landscape depression in which ponded water percolates through the soil to recharge an underlying aquifer.

    - ✓ **Bioswales** – Swales, shallow ditches, removing water from yards designed with deep, organic, porous soils and planted into dense vegetation to slow down runoff, promoting infiltration and trapping sediment.

Summary

Urban soils are found in generally populated areas. They can be composed of mostly inorganic soil. Characteristics vary with landscape and are changed through movement, compaction, storage, aeration or water damage. Changes also occur through human intervention. Many processes in urban settings affect soil such as cut and fill operations, buried debris, compaction and contamination. The EPA defines Brownfields. Cleaning up these areas protects the environment. Site planning is necessary to reduce pollution and clean up the environment. Modified and structured soils are composed of existing soil or created with additional amendments. Urban soil erosion control is important to keep runoff and sedimentation regulated. Vegetation helps in the control of urban soils and to maintain zero-runoff. Several options for keeping water contained are reusing for irrigation and a recharge source, wetlands and bioswales.

Additional Resources

Ashman, M.R. and G. Puri. 2002. Essential soil science. Ames, IA: Blackwell Publishing.

Parker, R. 2010. Plant and soil science. Clifton Park, NY: Delmar Publishing

Soil and Water Conservation Society
http://www.swcs.org/

Soil Science Society of America
https://www.soils.org/

US Department of Agriculture / National Resources Conservation Service
http://www.nrcs.usda.gov/wps/portal/nrcs/main/soils/use/urban/

Evaluation of Urban Soils
http://water.epa.gov/infrastructure/greeninfrastructure/upload/Evaluation-of-Urban-Soils.pdf

NRCS:Urban Soil Primer
http://www.nrcs.usda.gov/Internet/FSE_DOCUMENTS/nrcs142p2_052835.pdf

Brownfield Overview and Definition
http://www.epa.gov/brownfields/brownfield-overview-and-definition

Assessment

 Take the online assessment here: https://goo.gl/yDV3ce
Download and print the expanded written assessment by scanning this QR code or by going to this URL: https://www.tagmydoc.com/Ch19SS

Notes:

20 Government Agencies and Programs

Major Concept

Government, state and local agencies and programs assist agriculturists with education, research, management, technical help and financial assistance.

Objectives

- Identify the president that established the USDA
- Name five departments within the USDA
- Define five programs or services offered within the USDA
- Identify the USDA department that helps to fund research, education and extension at the state and local level
- Name the department that administers farm commodities, crop insurance and emergency assistance programs to farmers and ranchers
- Name the department that works to ensure adequate and high-quality of food
- List four areas in which the SWCD assists
- Name the agency which established the Clean Water Act
- Define three programs/activities that the NRCS conducts
- Name the USDA department that conducts the Wetlands Reserve Program
- Define the role of the National Association of Conservation Districts (NACD)

Key Terms

- Agricultural Research Service (ARS)
- Conservation Reserve Program (CRP)
- Environmental Quality Incentives Program (EQIP)
- Farm Service Agency (FSA)
- National Association of Conservation Districts (NACD)
- National Institute of Food and Agriculture (NIFA)
- Natural Resources Conservation Service (NRCS)
- Soil and Water Conservation Districts (SWCD)
- United States Department of Agriculture (USDA)

Chapter Resources

 Complementary full color illustrations, photos, charts and graphs are available by scanning this QR code or by following this URL: https://www.tagmydoc.com/SS20 These digital resources will enhance your understanding of the chapter concepts.

Government Agencies and Programs

- A myriad of agencies within the United States government cover all areas of agriculture and related topics – the USDA being the main agency.

- Information is offered in a variety of formats starting with advice from a county extension agent to a piece of paper to technical website downloads of information, webcasts, podcasts, workshops, online resources, county and state agencies, all working in conjunction with local growers.

- The availability of information is presented to keep the agriculturalist informed with local, state and government policies and updated techniques to assist with their area of need.

- Only a few of these agencies will be discussed in this chapter:

  o Agricultural Research Service (**ARS**)

  o Animal and Plant Health Inspection Service (**APHIS**)

  o Farm Service Agency (**FSA**)

  o Conservation Reserve Program (**CRP**) (with Farm Service Agency)

  o National Institute of Food and Agriculture (**NIFA**)

  o Natural Resources Conservation Service (**NRCS**)

United States Department of Agriculture (USDA)

- Founded in 1862, President Abraham Lincoln signed into law an act of Congress establishing the United States Department of Agriculture.

  o Two and one-half years later, in what would be his final annual message to the Congress; Lincoln called USDA "The People's Department." At that time, about half of all Americans lived on farms, compared with about 2 % today. But through work on food, agriculture, economic development, science, natural resource conservation and a host of issues, USDA still fulfills Lincoln's vision - touching the lives of every American, every day.

- The U.S. Department of Agriculture (USDA) is made up of 29 agencies and offices with nearly 100,000 employees who serve the American people at more than 4,500 locations across the country and abroad. The programs and services of the USDA include:

- Assisting rural communities

- Conservation

- Education and research

- Food and nutrition

- Marketing and trade

- Operations of the USDA includes:

    - Providing leadership on food, agriculture, natural resources, rural development, nutrition, and related issues based on public policy, the best available science, and effective management.

    - Creating the vision is to provide economic opportunity through innovation, helping rural America to thrive;

    - Promoting agriculture production that better nourishes Americans while also helping feed others throughout the world;

    - Preserving our Nation's natural resources through conservation, restored forests, improved watersheds, and healthy private working lands.

- The USDA maintains an extensive up-to-date website with resources for all programs and services - http://www.usda.gov/wps/portal/usda/usdahome

    - The information offered in this chapter is only a fraction of what is available on their website.

Agricultural Research Service (ARS)

- The Agricultural Research Service (ARS) works to ensure that Americans have reliable, adequate supplies of high-quality food and other agricultural products. ARS accomplishes its goals through scientific discoveries that help solve problems in crop and livestock production and protection, human nutrition, and the interaction of agriculture and the environment.

- Research programs within national programs

- 2,000 scientists and post docs

- 6,000 other employees

- Mission statement: "*ARS conducts research to develop and transfer solutions to agricultural problems of high national priority and provide information access and dissemination to: Ensure high quality, safe food, and other agricultural products; assess the nutritional needs of Americans; sustain a competitive agricultural economy; enhance the natural resource base and the environment and provide economic opportunities for rural citizens, communities, and society as a whole.*"

Animal and Plant Health Inspection Service (APHIS)

- APHIS' Plant Protection and Quarantine (PPQ) program safeguards U.S. agriculture and natural resources against the entry, establishment, and spread of economically and environmentally significant pests, and facilitates the safe trade of agricultural products

Farm Service Agency (FSA)

- The Farm Service Agency (FSA) ensures the well-being of American agriculture, the environment, and the American public through the administration of farm commodity programs; farm ownership, operating, and emergency loans; conservation and environmental programs; emergency and disaster assistance; and domestic and  international food assistance. FSA programs are delivered through an extensive network of field offices in 2,248 USDA County Service Centers and 51 State Offices.

- The Farm Service Agency (FSA) administers farm commodity, crop insurance, credit, environmental, conservation, and emergency assistance programs for farmers and ranchers.

- Programs within the FSA are: Farm Loan Programs, Disaster Assistance, Price Support; Conservation Programs, Daily Market Prices, and Commodity Procurement.

  o The FSA oversees many voluntary conservation-related programs. These include drinking water protection, deducing soil erosion, wildlife habitat preservation, preservation and restoration of forests and wetlands, aiding farmers whose farms are damaged by natural disasters.

  o **Conservation Reserve Program (CRP)** is a land conservation program administered by the Farm Service Agency (FSA). In exchange for a yearly rental payment, farmers enrolled in the program agree to remove environmentally sensitive land from agricultural production and plant species that will improve environmental health and quality. Contracts for land enrolled in CRP are 10-15 years in length. The long-term goal of the program is to re-establish valuable land cover to help improve water quality, prevent soil erosion, and reduce loss of wildlife habitat.

- FSA administers many funding programs and two major soil conservation programs. Many FSA activities administered at the state and local level by committees of local growers in Soil and Water Conservation Districts (SWCD).

National Institute of Food and Agriculture (NIFA)

- NIFA's unique mission is to advance knowledge for agriculture, the environment, human health and well-being, and communities by supporting research, education, and extension programs in the Land-Grant University System and other partner organizations. NIFA does not perform actual research, education, and extension but rather helps fund it at the state and local level and provides program leadership in these areas.

- The National Institute of Food and Agriculture (NIFA) is an agency within the U.S. Department of Agriculture (USDA), part of the executive branch of the Federal Government. Congress created NIFA through the Food, Conservation, and Energy Act of 2008. NIFA replaced the former Cooperative State Research, Education, and Extension Service (CSREES), which had been in existence since 1994.

- NIFA programs propel cutting-edge discoveries from research laboratories to farms, classrooms, communities, and back again. Through three main federal-funding mechanisms, NIFA supports programs that address key national challenge areas. Programs funded jointly by state and federal dollars. Personnel, in all areas of agriculture, may have extension appointments, research appointments, teaching positions at a college/university, or some combination. Extension services publish informational bulletins, run workshops, and provide expert advice specific to the state served.

- Within NIFA are Natural Resource/Soil programs. NIFA is involved in a diverse range of research, education, and outreach activities to better understand, maintain, and restore the health of this vital natural resource. Other resources are the National Cooperative Soil Survey, and the Web Soil Survey.

Natural Resources Conservation Service (NRCS)

- NRCS's natural resources conservation programs help people reduce soil erosion, enhance water supplies, improve water quality, increase wildlife habitat, and reduce damages caused by floods and other natural disasters.

- NRCS has a varied list of programs and activities, many involving some aspect of conservation, environmental, and water issues. These programs cover soil erosion, fertilizer, pest management, soil quality, etc.

- Replaced the older Soil Conservation Service established by Congress in 1935 to carry out a national program of soil and water conservation.

- NRCS Conservation Programs: Complete listings of currently available programs are on the Natural Resources Conservation Service website. Below are just a few of the programs/initiatives offered by the NRCS:

  o Mississippi River Basin Healthy Watersheds Initiative

  o Great Lakes Restoration Initiative

  o Conservation Technical Assistance Program and Activities

  o Environmental Improvement Programs

  o Stewardship Programs

  o National Watershed Programs

  o Easement Programs

  o Community Assistance Programs and Activities

  o Conservation Issues and Strategies

  o Resource Inventory and Assessment

  o Compliance, Appeals, Mediation, Relief

  o International Programs

Chapter
Resource

- For the most current Farm Bill information, visit the NRCS website. More information on programs, financial assistance, easements, partnerships and other resources are available on the web page.

- Characterized as cost-sharing programs, conservation compliance programs and conservation reserve programs.

  o **Environmental Quality Incentives Program (EQIP)**

    ✓ Provides financial and technical assistance to agricultural producers to address natural resource concerns and deliver environmental benefits such as improved water and air quality, conserved ground and surface water, reduced soil erosion and sedimentation or improved or created wildlife habitat.

- ○ **Conservation Stewardship Program** (CSP)

    - ✓ Helps agricultural producers maintain and improve their existing conservation systems and adopt additional conservation activities to address priority resources concerns. Participants earn CSP payments for conservation performance—the higher the performance, the higher the payment.

- ○ **Agricultural Management Assistance Program (AMA)**

    - ✓ Helps agricultural producers use conservation to manage risk and solve natural resource issues through natural resources conservation. NRCS administers the AMA conservation provisions while the Agricultural Marketing Service and the Risk Management Agency implement other provisions under AMA.

Soil and Water Conservation Districts or Commissions

- • Known in various parts of the country as "soil and water conservation districts," "resource conservation districts," "natural resource districts," "land conservation committees" and similar names, they share a single mission: to coordinate assistance from all available sources—public and private, local, state and federal—to develop locally-driven solutions to natural resource concerns.

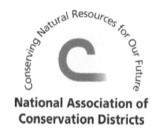

National Association of Conservation Districts

- • **National Association of Conservation Districts (NACD)** is a nonprofit organization that represents America's 3,000 conservation districts and the individuals who serve on their governing boards. Conservation districts are local units of government established under state law to carry out natural resource management programs at the local level. Districts work with millions of cooperating landowners and operators to help them manage and protect land and water resources on all private lands and many public lands in the United States.

- • Most will provide the following assistance:

    - ○ Implement farm, ranch and forestland conservation practices to protect soil productivity, water quality and quantity, air quality and wildlife habitat;

    - ○ Conserve and restore wetlands, which purify water and provide habitat for birds, fish and numerous other animals;

    - ○ Protect groundwater resources;

- o Assist communities and homeowners to plant trees and other land cover to hold soil in place, clean the air, provide cover for wildlife and beautify neighborhoods

- o Help developers control soil erosion and protect water and air quality during construction

- o Reach out to communities and schools to teach the value of natural resources and encourage conservation efforts

- o More than 17,000 citizens serve in elected or appointed positions on conservation districts' governing boards. The districts work directly with millions of cooperating land managers nationwide to manage and protect natural resources.

- Because conservation districts are established under state laws, they vary in what they are called and how they are funded. What is referred to as "conservation districts" are referred to by several other names under various state laws.

Conservation and Wetland Reserve Programs (CRP)

- The Wetlands Reserve Program (WRP) was a voluntary program that offered landowners the opportunity to protect, restore, and enhance wetlands on their property.

- The USDA Natural Resources Conservation Service (NRCS) provided technical and financial support to help landowners with their wetland restoration efforts through WRP.

- This program offered landowners an opportunity to establish long-term conservation and wildlife practices and protection.

- The goal of NRCS was to achieve the greatest wetland functions and values, along with optimum wildlife habitat, on every acre enrolled in the program.

  - o Natural Resources Conservation Service – Wetland Reserve Program
    http://www.nrcs.usda.gov/wps/portal/nrcs/detail/soils/survey/?cid=nrcs143_008419

- The Agricultural Conservation Easement Program (ACEP) provides financial and Technical assistance to help conserve agricultural lands and wetlands and their related benefits.

  - o Easements – Protecting and Enhancing our Natural Resources
    http://www.nrcs.usda.gov/wps/portal/nrcs/detail/or/programs/easements/acep/?cid=stelprdb1249312

- The Food Security Act of 1985, as amended, requires producers participating in most programs administered by the Farm Service Agency (FSA) and the Natural Resources Conservation Service (NRCS) to abide by certain conditions on any land owned or farmed that is highly erodible or that is considered a wetland.

- Natural Resources and Environment page within the Economic Research Service program has several conservation programs: working-land programs, land retirement program, easement programs, and conservation technical assistance program.

Environmental Protection Agency

- The main role of the EPA is to protect human health and the environment.

- The Clean Water Act (CWA) establishes the basic structure for regulating discharges of pollutants into the waters of the United States and regulating quality standards for surface waters. The basis of the CWA was enacted in 1948 and was called the Federal Water Pollution Control Act, but the Act was significantly reorganized and expanded in 1972. "Clean Water Act" became the Act's common name with amendments in 1972.

State and Local Efforts

- Most state and local agricultural departments can be located by searching [State] State Department of Agriculture.

- State & Local Government websites have links to each state's Department of Agriculture.

- Through extension, land-grant colleges and universities bring vital, practical information to agricultural producers, small business owners, consumers, families, and young people on a local level. https://nifa.usda.gov/extension

- Extension is an interactive learning environment delivering research-based information emerging from America's land-grant university system. It allows the user to locate university extensions in their area.

Summary

The USDA was founded in 1862. President Abraham Lincoln signed into law an act of Congress establishing the United States Department of Agriculture. Lincoln called USDA "The People's Department." At that time, about half of all Americans lived on farms, compared with about 2 % today. But through their work on food, agriculture, economic development, science, natural resource conservation and a host of issues, USDA still fulfills Lincoln's vision - touching the lives of every American, every day. The USDA maintains an extensive up-to-date website with resources for all programs and services. The best way to become familiar with all the USDA has to offer is to spend time on the website - http://www.usda.gov/wps/portal/usda/usdahome

Additional Resources

United States Department of Agriculture
http://www.usda.gov/wps/portal/usda/usdahome

Agricultural Research Service
http://www.ars.usda.gov/main/main.htm

National Institute of Food and Agriculture
https://nifa.usda.gov/

United States Department of Agriculture - Farm Service Agency
http://www.fsa.usda.gov/

Natural Resource Conservation Service
http://www.nrcs.usda.gov/wps/portal/nrcs/site/national/home/

U.S. Environmental Protection Agency
http://cfpub.epa.gov/

Economic Research Service
https://www3.epa.gov/

Assessment

Take the online assessment here: https://goo.gl/E2qjQs
Download and print the expanded written assessment by scanning this QR code or by going to this URL: https://www.tagmydoc.com/Ch20SS

Glossary

A

acid soil - A low pH is caused by the percolation of mildly acidic water; exchangeable bases are replaced by hydrogen ions.

acidic - Soil containing more hydrogen ions (H+) than hydroxyl ions (OH-).

acre-foot - Equal to approximately 326,000 gallons, or enough water to cover an acre of land one foot deep.

acre-inch - Water measured over a given area of one acre.

actinomycete - Group of organisms with characteristics between bacteria and fungi (often called mold bacteria).

adhesion - The force of attraction between unlike molecules (water to soil particles).

adobe - A mixture of sand, clay, water and sometimes a fibrous or organic material, has been used for buildings for thousands of years.

adsorption - A surface function where plants take nutrients out of the soil solution and store the nutrients.

aggregates - Groups of soil particles that bind to each other more strongly than to adjacent particles.

Agricultural Research Service (ARS) - Works to ensure that Americans have reliable, adequate supplies of high-quality food and other agricultural products. ARS accomplishes its goals through scientific discoveries that help solve problems in crop and livestock production and protection, human nutrition, and the interaction of agriculture and the environment.

agro-forestry - A type of land management combining trees with agricultural crops and/or animals.

alkaline - Soil containing more hydroxyl ions (OH-) than hydrogen ions (H+).

alkaline (soil) - A high pH is caused by reaction of water and the bases: calcium, magnesium, sodium, to form hydroxyl ions.

allelopathy - A chemical substance released by one plant that can benefit or inhibit the growth of another plant.

alluvial fan - A fan-shaped sediment deposit usually found at the base of a mountain range or hill.

alluvial soils - Soils deposited by fresh running water, such as rivers, which form sediments.

anion - Negatively charged atoms or molecules.

antitranspirants - Coating leaves with a chemical material that reduces water loss through stomata and leaf surfaces by reducing the size and number of stomata.

aquifer - Underground layers of rock and sediment saturated with water; water exists in most places under the earth's surface

arable land - Land suitable for crop production.

autotroph - Organisms that produce their own food, i.e. plants.

B
_____

banding - Narrow bands of fertilizer are applied in furrows two inches from seeds or seeding and two inches deep.

base saturation - Percentage of the cation exchange sites filled with exchangeable bases.

Best Management Practices (BMP) - A practice, or combination of practices, that is determined to be an effective and practicable (including technological, economic, and institutional considerations) means of preventing or reducing the amount of pollution generated by nonpoint sources to a level compatible with water quality goals.

biological weathering - Occurs when plants and biological life contribute to the disintegration of rocks.

bioremediation - The use of living things to reduce pollution; seeding with soil bacteria to break down organic pollutants.

biosolids - Nutrient-rich organic materials resulting from the treatment of domestic sewage in a treatment facility.

bioswales - Swales, shallow ditches, removing water from yards designed with deep, organic, porous soils and planted into dense vegetation to slow down runoff, promoting infiltration and trapping sediment.

broadcasting - Fertilizer is spread uniformly over the field before planting; occurs by use of machinery or aircraft.

brownfield - Brownfield sites; real property, the expansion, redevelopment, or reuse of which may be complicated by the presence or potential presence of a hazardous substance, pollutant, or contaminant"

buffering - Occurs when the soil solution contains either a weak acid and its salt or a weak base and its salt, which is resistant to changes in pH.

buffering capacity - The capacity of a soil to resist change in pH.

bulk density - Refers to the weight of the oven–dry (moisture removed) soil with its natural structural arrangement.

burned lime - Or quicklime, is made by heating limestone; heat drives off carbon dioxide resulting in the lighter calcium oxide:

C

calcareous soils - Soils in a very high alkaline range that are 100% base-saturated and contain several percent or more of calcium carbonate.

Calcium Carbonate Equivalent (CCE) - Expression of the acid-neutralizing capacity of a carbonate rock relative to that of pure calcium carbonate.

capillarity - The tendency of a liquid in a capillary tube or absorbent material to rise or fall as a result of surface tension.

carbon cycle - Plants remove carbon dioxide from the atmosphere and oceans by fixing it into glucose; in turn, animals, plants and human activities produce carbon dioxide (CO_2) by respiration, decomposition and burning which is used by photosynthesis.

carbon-nitrogen ratio or **(C:N Ratio)** - A ratio of the mass of carbon to the mass of nitrogen in a substance.

cation - A positively charged atom or molecule.

cation exchange capacity (CEC) - Total number of exchangeable cations a soil can adsorb.

chemical weathering - Occurs when changes in the chemical makeup of rock is altered causing it to soften and/or break down. This type of weathering occurs mostly in hot and humid environments.

cohesion - The force of attraction between like molecules (water molecules to other water molecules).

colluvium - Material that slides/rolls down slopes and accumulates at the bottom (land slide).

complete fertilizer- A fertilizer that contains the three primary nutrients: Nitrogen (N), Phosphorus (P) and Potassium (K).

composite sample - A sample comprising two or more increments selected to represent the material being analyzed.

compost - When organic material is stored in a pile on the ground under conditions that increase decay.

concrete - A material made of crushed stone, rock, sand and cement. Cement is a fine powder made of limestone, silicon, aluminum, iron and clay and mixed with water. When water is added, cement hardens.

Conservation Reserve Program (CRP) - A land conservation program administered by the Farm Service Agency (FSA).

conservation tillage - A method that leaves the previous year's crop residue on a field from before and after planting a crop to reduce soil erosion and runoff.

consumptive use - The total water used to produce a crop – including evaporation, transpiration and water that become part of the plant.

continuous cropping - The production of a single crop in a field.

conventional tillage - A process of cultivating the soil to prepare a seedbed and for weed control. A sequence of events is used such as ploughing and harrowing and removal of plant residue from previous crops.

core aeration - Mechanically removing plugs of soil and thatch from a lawn.

cover crop - Planting used mainly to slow erosion and improve soil fertility.

crop rotation - The growing of selected crops in a regular order on any field.

cropping system - A total of all crops and the sequences and/or management practices used to grow those crops; proper soil management necessary to maintain or increase productivity of the crops.

cultivation on the contour - The practice of planting and cultivating of crops following the contours of the land.

D

deltas - The alluvial deposit at the mouth of a river, i.e. Mississippi Delta.

denitrification - The loss or removal of nitrogen or nitrogen compounds; specifically: reduction of nitrates or nitrites commonly by bacteria (as in soil) that usually results in the escape of nitrogen into the air

detritus - Active soil organic matter.

double cropping - or sequential cropping; planting a second crop immediately following the harvest of the first crop (also considered multiple cropping).

drainage - The natural or artificial removal of surface and sub-surface water from a given area.

dryland farming - The profitable production of crops without irrigation or very limited, variable or unstable rainfall.

E

emitters - Device with pin-hole size openings located at intervals along lateral plastic tubes laid on soil surface.

Environmental Quality Incentives Program (EQIP) - Provides financial and technical assistance to agricultural producers to address natural resource concerns and deliver environmental benefits such as improved water and air quality, conserved ground and surface water, reduced soil erosion and sedimentation or improved or created wildlife habitat.

eolian deposits - Wind-transported parent material.

eutrophication - An increase of algae growth in water bodies. In many ecosystems; this is a slow, long term, but natural process.

exchangeable bases - Some cations not held very strongly and can be easily exchanged.

F

fallow - Plowed land left without a crop growing for a season.

family - Families are established within a subgroup based on properties important to plant growth and soil uses such as texture, temperature, mineralogy and soil depth. Name composed of descriptive words placed before subgroup name.

Farm Service Agency (FSA) - Administers farm commodity, crop insurance, credit, environmental, conservation, and emergency assistance programs for farmers and ranchers.

fertigation - Fertilizer is added to irrigation water and applied to crops at intervals during the growing season.

fertilizer - Any material applied to a soil or plant to supply essential elements.

fertilizer grade - An expression referring to the legal guarantee of the available plant nutrients expressed as a percentage by weight in a fertilizer, e.g. a 12-32-16 grade of NPK complex.

fertilizer ratio - Indicates a comparative proportion of nitrogen to phosphate to potash. For example, a 15-10-5 fertilizer has a ratio of 3-2-1, and an 8-12-4 fertilizer has a ratio of 2-3-1.

Field capacity (FC) - The amount of soil moisture or water content held in the soil after excess water has drained away and the rate of downward movement has decreased.

fillers - May be sand, clay granules, ground limestone or ground corncobs and are used to bring a load of bulk fertilizer to a weight of 1 ton.

floodplains - An area of low-lying ground adjacent to a river, formed mainly of river sediments and subject to flooding.

fluid fertilizer - Concentrated fertilizers that must be diluted with water; available in liquid form, powder, or pellets.

foliar feeding - Nutrients are applied to the plant itself by using diluted fertilizer solutions that are sprayed on crop leaves.

frost wedging - Occurs in cold climates when water freezes and expands in rocks. The action of expanding and contracting causes the rock to crack peeling outer layers away (exfoliation).

fungi - More complex, non-photosynthetic, multi-celled organisms (except yeast, which is single celled).

furrow-diking - Special equipment creates basins to hold water by making furrows with dikes (small ridges).

furrow method - Water flows in furrows along contours or straight furrows; used in row crops. This method is efficient in water utilization.

G

Geographic Information System (GIS) - Computerized data management system designed to capture, store, analyze, manage and display spatial and geographical information such as maps and reports.

glacial drifts - Material, as gravel, sand, or clay, transported and deposited by a glacier or by glacial meltwater.

Global Positioning Systems (GPS) - Allows instant identification of location with precise satellite coordinates; replaces need to estimate location using printed maps and identifiable landmarks.

granules - Treated, evenly sized grains, spread evenly and easily, coated to reduce moisture absorption during storage.

gravitational potential - When soil water is above water table level and carries potential energy by gravity.

gravitational water - Moves into, through or out of the soil under the influence of gravity; found in the macropores; moves rapidly out of well-drained soil (two to three days); can cause flooding in other areas; occupies air space in the pore spaces, can deprive oxygen to roots, causing plants to wilt and even die.

great group - Each suborder is divided into great groups based on similar layers present in horizons with emphasis on presence or absence of specific diagnostic features, base status, soil temperature and soil moisture regimes. Named by adding prefix to suborder name.

green manure - Crops grown for a specific period and plowed under before maturing to improve soil fertility and quality.

groundwater - Water than has seeped into the ground through rocks, cracks and soil.

guaranteed analysis - The minimum amount of N, P_2O_5, K_2O, etc. in the fertilizer material.

H

heterotroph - Break down complex organic compounds into simpler compounds, release energy by oxidizing carbon and hydrogen atoms, producing carbon dioxide and water.

horizons - Designated according to their soil profile position and the varying physical and chemical processes that created them.

humification - Compounds formed from chemical reaction with soil nitrogen that is large, rich in nitrogen, highly complex and resistant to attack.

humus - Stable organic matter left in soil when plants or animals die.

hydrologic (water) cycle - Continually moves water from the soil to the plants then to the atmosphere and back to the soil.

hydrophilic gel polymers - Increase water-holding capacity of soil; absorb and hold water many times their weight, not releasing it until soil has dried.

hydrophobic - Repels water instead of absorbing it.

hydroseeding - A planting process that uses a slurry of seed and mulch. It is often used as an erosion control technique on construction sites, as an alternative to the traditional process of broadcasting or sowing dry seed.

hygroscopic water - Water absorbed from the atmosphere and held very tightly by the soil particles, so that it is unavailable to plants in amounts sufficient for them to survive.

hypoxia - Severe, extreme low-oxygen conditions.

I-J-K

immobilization - The conversion of inorganic compounds to organic compounds by micro-organisms or plants, by which it is prevented from being accessible to plants.

infiltration - The movement of water into soil.

inoculation - Beneficially infecting soil with useful organisms.

intercropping - or relay cropping; growing two or more generally dissimilar crops simultaneously on the same piece of land; grown in distinct rows.

irrigation - The artificial application of water to soil to supplement water available from rainfall and snow to help with crop production.

L

land capability classification - A system of grouping soils on the basis of their "capability" to produce common cultivated crops and pasture plants without deteriorating over a long period of time.

landscaping - The care and maintenance of a landscape or ornamental plantings.

leaching - Dissolved substances can pass through soil by rainwater or irrigation, which causes the loss of water-soluble plant nutrients.

legumes - Nitrogen fixing plants grown for seed value such as alfalfa and peanuts.

levees - Ridges of sediment deposited naturally alongside a river. These can be through flooding or manmade to regulate water flow.

lignin - Makes up most of soil humus; large, highly complex molecules, 10-30% of plant tissue; makes plants rigid and decay resistant

liming - Materials contain calcium and/or magnesium in forms, which when dissolved, will neutralize soil acidity.

load-bearing capacity - The capacity of soil to support the loads applied to the ground.

logarithmic scale - The pH scale is logarithmic and as a result, each whole pH value below 7 is ten times more acidic than the next higher value.

M

macrofauna - Animals that are one centimeter or more long but smaller than an earthworm.

macronutrients - Chemical elements required in large amounts for plant growth and development.

map units - A collection of areas defined and named the same in terms of their soil components and/or miscellaneous areas.

matric potential - Results from the attraction of water molecules to soil particles; determines movement of soil water and water availability to plants.

mesofauna - Typically live within soil pores, have limited burrowing ability (mostly inhabit surface litter) and feed on organic materials, microflora, microfauna and other invertebrates.

micelle - A particle of silicate clay.

microfauna - The smallest of soil organisms and have to be viewed with a microscope.

microflora - Bacteria and microscopic algae and fungi, especially those living in a particular site or habitat.

micro-irrigation - The frequent application of small quantities of water directly above and below the soil surface

micronutrients - Minute amounts of these seven essential elements are found in plants and soils, but their roles are critical for plant nutrition.

mineral cycle - Processes that regulates the flow, distribution, and migration of mineral nutrients across the Earth's surface. Minerals are naturally occurring chemical compounds that are made up of elements.

mineralization - The decomposition or oxidation of the chemical compounds in organic matter releasing the nutrients contained in those compounds into soluble inorganic forms that may be plant-accessible.

mixed fertilizer - A fertilizer that contains two or more nutrients; may be created by mixing two different "straight" fertilizers together.

monocropping - or monoculture – production of a single crop in a field.

mottled - Spotted or blotched

muck - Organic material that is rotten, highly decomposed; often slimy and black in color.

mulch till - A process where crop residue is spread uniformly over a field to aid in planting the next crop; accomplished by minimum tillage such as chiseling and disk harrowing to partially incorporate surface organic matter.

multiple cropping - Growing two or more crops consecutively or at the same time on the same field in the same year; crops needed that mature quickly to allow two harvests in one year.

mycorrhizae - Fungi that form a symbiotic (mutually beneficial) relationship with plant roots and help with plant growth.

N

National Association of Conservation Districts (NACD) - A nonprofit organization that represents America's 3,000 conservation districts and the individuals who serve on their governing boards. Conservation districts are local units of government established under state law to carry out natural resource management programs at the local level.

National Institute of Food and Agriculture (NIFA) - An agency within the U.S. Department of Agriculture (USDA), part of the executive branch of the Federal Government. Congress created NIFA through the Food, Conservation, and Energy Act of 2008. NIFA replaced the former Cooperative State Research, Education, and Extension Service (CSREES), which had been in existence since 1994.

Natural Resources Conservation Service (NRCS) - Formerly known as the Soil Conservation Service is an agency of the United States Department of Agriculture that provides technical assistance to farmers and other private landowners and managers.

Near-infrared Spectroscopy (NIRS) - A method that uses the near infrared region of the electromagnetic spectrum (from about 800 nm to 2500 nm). This method, typically used in the medical field, is now being used in soil analysis.

necrotic - The death of most or all the cells or tissue due to disease.

nematode - The most numerous multicellular animals on earth. A handful of soil will contain thousands of the microscopic worms, many of them parasites of insects, plants or animals.

neutral - When a soil contains equal concentrations of hydrogen and hydroxyl ions.

nitrification - The biological oxidation of ammonia or ammonium to nitrite followed by the oxidation of the nitrite to nitrate. Nitrification is an important step in the nitrogen cycle in soil.

nitrogen cycle - This is the movement and exchange of organic and inorganic matter back into the production of living matter.

nitrogen fixation - Part of the nitrogen cycle. Before nitrogen can be used by plants, it must first be removed from the atmosphere – either naturally through nitrogen fixation, which occurs in green plants called legumes or commercially through fertilizer plants. Nitrogen fixation is the process whereby elemental nitrogen is removed from the atmosphere by soil bacteria called rhizobia.

nonpoint source pollution - Usually comes from land runoff, precipitation, drainage, and seepage.

no-till - A way of growing crops or pasture from year to year without disturbing the soil through tillage; considered a type of conservation tillage; more many advantages than disadvantages.

O

olericulture - A branch of horticulture that deals with the production, storage, processing, and marketing of vegetables.

order - Based on presence or absence of key layers in the diagnostic horizon. The differences relate to dominant soil forming processes and degree of soil formation. Each order is identified by a word ending in 'sol.'

organic farming - A farming method that involves growing and nurturing crops without the use of synthetic based fertilizers and pesticides.

organic matter - Plant and animal material, both dead and living.

organic standards - Indicates the food or other agricultural product has been produced through approved methods. Specific requirements are verified by USDA-accredited certifying agents before labeled as USDA organic.

osmotic potential - Refers to the attraction of salts and dissolved organic compounds (solutes) to water.

P-Q

parent material - The underlying geological material (generally bedrock or a superficial or drift deposit) in which soil horizons form.

peat - A brown, soil-like material characteristic of boggy, acid ground, consisting of partly decomposed vegetable matter. It is widely cut and dried for use in gardening and as fuel.

pedology - The study of the formation and classification of soil.

pedon - A unit of soil, typically one meter by one meter in width and 1.5 meters deep (extending to the root depth).

pelletized lime - Finely ground limestone, pelletized with the aid of clay or other type of synthetic binder.

penetrometer - An instrument for determining the consistency or hardness of a substance by measuring the depth or rate of penetration of a rod or needle driven into it by a known force.

percolation - The downward movement of water within the soil.

perlite - Large granules of light-weight expanded volcanic glass.

Permanent Wilting Point (PWP) - The point where no more water is available to the plant.

permeability - The quality of soil allowing both kinds of water movement.

pH - A figure expressing the acidity or alkalinity of a solution on a logarithmic scale on which 7 is neutral, lower values are more acid, and higher values more alkaline.

phosphorus index - Quantifies potential phosphorus hazards on lands, to identify sites with a higher risk of phosphorus movement and to help devise corrective plans.

plant tissue test - Plants themselves can be tested for nutrient content in order to determine fertilizer needs.

point source pollution - The Clean Water Act, is any discernible, confined and discrete conveyance, including but not limited to any pipe, ditch, channel, tunnel, conduit, well, discrete fissure, container, rolling stock, concentrated animal feeding operation, or vessel or other floating craft, from which pollutants are or may be discharged.

polyculture - Growing multiple crops in the same space; includes multiple cropping, intercropping, companion planting, beneficial weeds and alley cropping; can imitate the diversity of natural ecosystems.

pomology - The study and cultivation of fruits and nuts.

pop-up fertilizer - Also called seed placement, where a small amount of fertilizer is placed with the seeds during planting.

pore space - A part of the volume of soil measured for bulk density.

precipitation - Water released from clouds in the form of rain, freezing rain, sleet, snow or hail.

precision farming - An approach to farm management that uses information technology (IT) to ensure that the crops and soil receive exactly what they need for optimum health and productivity.

preferential flow - The flow of free water through large pores, bypassing the general soil matrix.

pressurized liquid fertilizer - Fertilizers held in pressurized tanks until they can be injected into the soil.

prills - Free of dust, smooth, round, easy to use and spread, coated to protect during storage.

primary consumer - They eat the primary producers.

primary producer - Organisms (for example: plants) that produce their own food. They are the base of the food chain.

primary tillage - Initially breaks up the soil after a harvest to a depth of approximately 10-12 inches and buries residue from a previous crop.

pulverized fertilizer - Finely crushed powder, difficult to spread evenly, may cake during storage.

R

rain-fed farming - The natural application of water to the soil through direct rainfall. This occurs in areas where there is enough precipitation to grow crops without irrigation. It is also common in poor, developing countries, where irrigation is not available.

rangeland - Those lands on which native vegetation is mostly grasses, grass-like plants, forbs (herbaceous flowering plant that is not a grass), or shrubs suitable for grazing or browsing; also includes woodlands and most deserts, shrublands, tundra, alpine communities, marshes and meadows.

recharge basins - Landscape depression in which ponded water percolates through the soil to recharge an underlying aquifer.

relay intercropping - Growing two or more crops simultaneously during part of each crop's life cycle; second crop planted after first crop has reached reproductive stage of growth but before it is ready for harvest.

residual soil - weather in place, weathering occurs slowly, are shallow and usually found on bedrock.

resistance block - A meter is used to read the electrical resistance of moisture blocks installed in the ground; the blocks incorporate two electrodes imbedded in a gypsum material and covered with a porous material; porous material allows water to move in equilibrium with the soil moisture indicating changes in amount of water in soil.

retention ponds - Manmade depressions installed to collect runoff water.

ridge-till - Maintaining ridges is essential; old residue removed into furrows in preparation for new crop; operating depth is shallow, disturbing only the ridge tops; some control of weeds and incorporation of herbicide possible.

root wedging - Occurs when roots grow into a crack in a rock and the pressure of this pries apart the stone.

rosetting - Circular arrangement of leaves.

rotation cropping - A cropping sequence that includes more than one crop over several years.

runoff - Excess water that flows over the ground.

saline - Salty

saline soils - Contain soluble salts and impairs productivity of plants but does not contain an excess of exchangeable sodium.

saline-sodic soil - Typically characterized by sodium (Na) saturation greater than 15% of the CEC and a pH of 8.4 or less.

salinization - The process by which water-soluble salts accumulate in the soil.

salt wedging - Occurs when salt is left behind after water evaporates and over time the salt creates pressure causing rocks to split and weaken.

saprophytes - Decomposers, feed on dead organic matter.

saturated flow - (gravitational) water flows downward by gravity; occurs mainly in large soil pores.

Scientific Irrigation Scheduling (SIS) - Refers to a method of irrigating that measures the actual soil moisture and crop evapotranspiration and delivers water to the crops based on those scientific measurements.

secondary consumers - Consume the primary consumers.

secondary tillage - Not as deep as primary tillage and creates a smoother finish to make a good seedbed.

series - Often named for a nearby town or landscape where first discovered. Consists of soils within a family that have similar color, texture, structure, reaction, mineral and chemical composition, and soil profile arrangement.

shrink-swell potential - Extent that a clay (smallest class of soil particles) soil will expand or contract when wet or dry.

side-dressing - Fertilizer is applied to the soil six to eight inches from the plants along the rows.

site-specific management - Individualized to small areas or "sites" to be tested and managed.

slag - Byproduct of steel manufacturing and valued as fertilizer in gardens and farms in some areas of the country because of the slowly-released phosphate content in phosphorus-containing slag, and its liming effect.

slow-release fertilizer - Designed to slowly release nutrients into the soil over many weeks or even months.

sod crops - Cover the ground surface and fill the surface soil with fibrous roots tend to hold the soil in place and reduce erosion.

sodic - or alkali soils contain excessive amounts of sodium (Na) on the soil CEC sites.

sodic soils - Exchangeable sodium percentage (or sodium saturation) is 15 or more, and pH is in the range 8.5 to 10.0. If soluble salts are not present, but exchangeable sodium is, the soil can be called "sodic". Sodic soils contain sufficient exchangeable sodium to interfere with the growth of most plants.

sodium adsorption ratio (SAR) - Compares the concentration of sodium ions with the concentration of calcium and magnesium.

soil - The soft material that covers the surface of the earth and provides a place for the growth of plant roots.

soil aggregates - Groups of soil particles that bind to each other more strongly than to adjacent particles.

Soil and Water Conservation Districts (SWCD) - Districts work in both urban and rural settings, with landowners and with other units of government, to carry out a program for the conservation, use, and development of soil, water, and related resources.

soil classification - The process of arranging soil into categories based on common properties and according to usage.

soil colloids - Tiny clay and humus particles carrying a slight electrical charge which attracts nutrient ions. Silicate clays, oxide clays and humus are three types of soil colloids.

soil erosion - The movement of soil particles from one place to another under the influence of water or wind

soil horizons - Designated according to their soil profile position and the varying physical and chemical processes that created them.

soil injection - Used to place liquid or gaseous fertilizer below the soil near the plants roots.

soil pitting - Creating tiny pits to capture water.

soil profile - A vertical section of soil from the ground surface downwards through all of its horizons to where the soil meets underlying rock.

soil sampling - A sample of the soil to be tested is collected and sent to a testing center.

soil survey - The systematic examination, description, classification and mapping of soils in an area.

soil taxonomy - A system of classifying soils based on observable and quantifiable properties that can be viewed and sampled. Soils are grouped according to physical, chemical and mineralogical properties present in their soil horizons.

soil test - Performed in a lab generally analyze pH, nitrogen, phosphorus, potassium, calcium, magnesium, sodium, sulfur and salinity. More detailed tests are available which measure micronutrients such as zinc, iron, copper, manganese and boron.

soil texture - Refers to the amount of sand, silt and clay in the soil.

soil texture triangle - Used to determine textural name of a soil by measuring percentage of sand, silt and clay present in soil.

soluble - Able to be dissolved, especially in water.

split application - Divide up the year's fertilizer needs into two or more parts and apply at each interval.

starter fertilizer - A small quantity of fertilizer nutrients applied near the seed at planting which enhances the development of emerging seedlings by supplying essential nutrients in accessible locations near the roots.

straight fertilizer - A fertilizer that contains only one nutrient.

strip cropping - Growing soil-conserving and soil-depleting crops in alternate strips running perpendicular to the slope of the land

strip-till - The method of making narrow rows of 8 to 10 inches wide where seeds will be planted, leaving the soil in between the rows untilled; is considered a form of no-till; requires special equipment.

structure - Refers to the arrangement of soil particles. A well-developed structure usually indicates the presence of clay.

subgroup - Determined based on how the properties fit the typical concept of its great group. Describes characteristics such as wetness, sand, etc. New name is added before the great group name.

suborder - Each soil order is divided into a suborder based on how they differ in wetness, climate, major parent material, vegetation and other factors.

subsoil - The layer of soil just under the topsoil.

surface water - Water that collects on the surface of the ground.

sustainable agriculture - A philosophy and collection of practices that seeks to protect resources while ensuring adequate productivity. It strives to minimize off-farm inputs like fertilizers and pesticides and to maximize on-farm resources like nitrogen fixation by legumes. Top yields are less a goal than optimum and profitable yields based on reduced input costs.

symbiont - Organisms that live with another organism in a partnership that is beneficial to both.

T

talus - Sand and rocks that collect at the foot of a slope.

Temporary Wilting Point (TWP) - When plants lose water faster than it can be absorbed; plants can recover when conditions improve.

tensiometer – A sealed, airtight, water-filled tube with a porous tip on one end and a vacuum gauge on the other end which measures soil water suction expressed as tension; also called potentiometer.

tension - A measure of how much suction the soil pore exerts on water.

terracing - The practice of constructing embankments or ridges across sloping soils.

tillage - preparation of the soil for a good seedbed growing environment.

tilth - The condition of tilled soil, especially in respect to suitability for sowing seeds.

topdressing - A type of surface broadcasting where fertilizer is spread over a growing crop and not mixed into the soil.

topsoil - The surface or very top layer of soil.

transpiration - Evaporative process where water turns to vapor and is released from plants through the stomata (tiny pores) in their leaves.

U-V

United States Department of Agriculture (USDA) - Providing leadership on food, agriculture, natural resources, rural development, nutrition, and related issues based on public policy, the best available science, and effective management.

unsaturated flow - Water flows primarily by capillary action (multi-directional) from moist to dry soil; or from areas of high potential to areas of low potential called capillary rise.

vermiculite - A yellow or brown mineral found as an alteration product of mica and other minerals, and used for insulation or as a moisture-retentive medium for growing plants.

vertical mulching - A technique that can be used to partially alleviate soil compaction within the critical root zones of trees. Soil compaction is harmful as it reduces the amount of pore space in the soil normally filled by oxygen (micro-pores) and water (macro-pores).

W-X-Y-Z

water erosion - Caused by raindrops, surface flow and gully flow. A selective process in which organic matter and finer soil particles are removed first which rapidly destroys productivity of cultivated land.

water holding capacity - The total amount of water soil can hold at field capacity. Sandy soils tend to have low water storage capacity.

water penetration - The depth to which irrigation water or rain penetrates the soil before the rate of downward movement becomes negligible.

water-use efficiency - Can be measured by the amount of water needed to produce a unit of dry plant matter.

weathering - The process by which rock is broken down into smaller pieces.

Web Soil Survey (WSS) - Provides soil data and information produced by the National Cooperative Soil Survey. It is operated by the USDA Natural Resources Conservation Service (NRCS) and provides access to the largest natural resource information system in the world.

wind erosion - Common in dry areas where soils are often bare of vegetation and high wind velocities are common.

xeriscaping - A type of landscaping that reduces or eliminates the use of water.

Soil Science Activities to Enhance Learning

Here is a list of free Internet activity resources that can be used in combination with this book:

Title	URL
Soils 4 Teachers – Lesson and Activities	http://www.soils4teachers.org/lessons-and-activities
Soils 4 Kids – Experiments and Hands-on Projects	http://www.soils4kids.org/experiments
Nutrients for Life – Science of Soil	http://www.thescienceofsoil.com/teacher-resources
Teaching Soil and Earth Science on Pinterest	https://www.pinterest.com/globeprogram/teaching-stem-the-scoop-on-soil-and-earth-science/
Dr. Dirt K-12 Resources	http://www.doctordirt.org/
Soil Net – Various Activities and Information	http://www.soil-net.com/
Dirt – Secrets of the Soil -Activity Booklet	http://utah.agclassroom.org/files/uploads/estore/unit_dirt.pdf
How Stuff Works – Soil Experiments	https://lifestyle.howstuffworks.com/crafts/other-arts-crafts/science-projects-for-kids-soil-experiments.htm
Soil Lab Modules – University of British Columbia	http://labmodules.soilweb.ca/
Soils 4 Youth Activities – Canada	http://soil4youth.soilweb.ca/activities/
Demonstrations in Soil Science – Purdue University	https://www.agry.purdue.edu/courses/agry255/brochure/brochure.PDF
Virtual Labs – A Variety of Labs including pH	http://virtuallabs.nmsu.edu/